The *Choosing to*
FORGIVE
W O R K B O O K

The *Choosing to* FORGIVE

W O R K B O O K

Les Carter, Ph.D. & Frank Minirth, M.D.

Authors of *The Anger Workbook*

THOMAS NELSON PUBLISHERS

AUTHOR'S NOTE: In the pages to follow you will notice that we refer to case illustrations. Although the essence of our illustrations is entirely real, we have taken great care to adjust the identifying elements of those illustrations to protect the confidentiality of those involved.

Published in Nashville, Tennessee, by Thomas Nelson, Inc.

Unless otherwise noted, Scripture quotations are from THE NEW KING JAMES VERSION. Copyright © 1979, 1980, 1982, 1990, Thomas Nelson, Inc.

ISBN 0-7852-8255-6

Printed in the United States of America.

8 9 10 11 HG 08 07 06 05

Contents

Preface

In today's world, not many things can be stated with absolute certainty, yet one thing is sure: As long as we live on this side of heaven, we will face conflict. As a result we will be susceptible to depression, anger, anxiety, broken relationships, rejection, and manipulation. It doesn't sound very appealing, does it?

In spite of such a disheartening thought, you should know that the two of us, Drs. Les Carter and Frank Minirth, are, by nature, optimists. Each working day of our lives we talk with people who have been on the losing end of conflicts, yet we intend to instill in each of them a sense of hope. Yes, conflict is inevitable. And yes, it hurts—sometimes very deeply. In spite of this bad news, though, humans are not without options. Although in life you may not be able to opt out of all of your bad circumstances, you still can choose your emotional and relationship patterns.

That's what this book is about—choices. Once you realize the choices available to you, it will be possible for you, too, to develop optimism. A patient at our clinic once realized out loud, "People may be able to control things that happen on the outside of me, but I've determined that I don't have to let them possess what lies on the inside of me." That was a major breakthrough for him because he had not always lived with such optimistic thinking. Once he understood his God-given freedom to choose personal direction, he was able to make the breakthroughs he so desperately needed and desired.

Our guess is that you are probably reading this book in the aftermath of an unwanted and undesirable hurt, rejection, or disappointment. Certainly you did not choose to be in those circumstances, yet there you were. Perhaps there have been times you've assumed a position of hopelessness, feeling stuck in your bitterness, discouragement, or cynicism. Our message to you is clear: You can afford to hope again, and you have choices that can carry you out of and away from the emotional pits.

Let us put your emotional stagnation into perspective. When you were fifteen or sixteen years old, how many times did a trusted guide sit down with you and say, "Let's discuss the meaning and direction of your emotions, how you handle adversity, and how you will respond to the inevitable conflicts of life"? If you are like most, this conversation never happened. The vast majority of people enter their adult years less than fully prepared for the emotional responses they will have in the aftermath of conflicts. That's not to say you weren't taught right from wrong. You've probably been told repeatedly that you're supposed to forgive others, to be kind, to remove from yourself a hateful spirit, and to be fair-minded. Now, however, you realize that being told what you should do is different from being trained in *how* to sift through the meaning and direction of your emotions.

In this workbook we will walk you through the steps needed to become aware of the emotions and needs that tend to accompany major hurts, and guide you toward the ultimate goal of forgiveness. We do not suppose for a minute that this process is simple or quick. Lots of thought and effort and prayer will be necessary as you work through the steps we have outlined. In fact, you may find it beneficial to stay in touch with an accountability partner who can help keep you on track in your efforts. That partner may be a spouse, a close friend, a minister, a professional counselor, or a group of laypeople who want to be a team of encouragers. Openly exploring your choices with others makes your commitment to solutions more powerful.

Know that before you ever heard of *The Choosing to Forgive Workbook*, we have prayed for you. Our desire is that God will put this book into the hands of people who can genuinely benefit from its teachings and insights. We have prayed that you will learn to choose the healthy patterns of life that cause you to disengage from the pain that has burdened you, ultimately finding the peace and confidence that accompany a forgiving spirit.

Read with a readiness to learn and a readiness to be challenged. Whatever problem precedes your study of forgiveness, it is not so great that it precludes your ability to choose.

Les Carter, Ph.D.
Frank Minirth, M.D.

Acknowledgments

We consider it a privilege to be partners with the team at Thomas Nelson Publishers. We are especially appreciative of the guidance that comes from Janet Thoma. Do you remember your toughest high school English teacher who would never let you get away with dangling participles and who always expected (and amazingly received) perfection from you? That teacher was probably somehow related to Janet. She is one of those rare people who expect the finest from others and are able to help them find it in themselves!

Also, a major thanks is due to Irene Swindell who, once again, has labored with us in the preparation of this manuscript. In the past she has taught some of the very materials she has typed for us to her women's Bible study classes. Perhaps now she's armed with even more teaching material. She is the epitome of a servant and we hope she continues to be blessed in her work because she is such a blessing to the lives she touches.

Twelve Steps to Forgiveness

Step 1. Openly recognize wrong deeds to be wrong deeds.

Step 2. Recognize that your anger is not only normal, but necessary.

Step 3. Realize how ongoing bitterness will ultimately hurt you.

Step 4. Learn from your problems by establishing better boundaries.

Step 5. Refuse to be in the inferior position and resist the desire to be superior.

Step 6. Avoid the futility of judgments, letting God be the ultimate judge.

Step 7. Allow yourself permission to grieve.

Step 8. Confront the injuring party if appropriate.

Step 9. Find emotional freedom as you let go of the illusion of control.

Step 10. Choose forgiveness because it is part of your life's mission.

Step 11. Come to terms with others' wrong deeds by recognizing your own need for forgiveness.

Step 12. Become a source of encouragement to other hurting people.

1

Clarify the Need for Forgiveness

Step 1. Openly recognize wrong deeds to be wrong deeds.

A look of defeat crossed Coleen's face as she spoke with Dr. Carter. "It's been over five years since Mark left me, but I'm still having trouble forgiving him. Every day I'm faced with reminders of the pain he caused me by running off with another woman."

In her early forties now, Coleen recalled how she and Mark had been college sweethearts. Both had attended a traditional liberal arts college and had been hailed as the ideal couple. Handsome in appearance, friends had assumed they would be the ones to epitomize marital bliss. Upon graduation, Mark got a better-than-average job with a cutting-edge company that offered many perks and opportunities for advancement. Mark proved to be a winner by rapidly climbing the ladder of success. Coleen had taught school for two years before becoming pregnant with the first of their two daughters. Because of Mark's success she was able to stay home to become a full-time mother and wife. "I really had a charmed life," she recalled.

But fourteen years into their marriage, Coleen realized something was strangely missing. Mark had ceased calling her each day from the office just to say a friendly hello. He suddenly had more meetings that required him to keep later hours than normal. When at home, Mark had become increasingly distant and quiet. Her intuition told her to expect trouble.

"I began suspecting an affair, so I started playing detective," she explained. "It didn't take long for me to discover some serious discrepancies in the reports of Mark's whereabouts. So one day I decided to follow him when he said he had to run an errand, and sure enough, my suspicions were confirmed. He'd been having an affair for several months with a woman from his office."

Dr. Carter listened intently as she described the agony of having to confront him only to hear him tell lie after lie. At her insistence they sought counseling, but this only added to her pain because he could not, would not, be honest with the counselor. Finally, he left the house, and within a few months they were divorced. Predictably, the legal process was ugly and adversarial.

"Even now I don't feel he realizes the damage he's done," she cried. "He doesn't have to face the aggravation brought on by two teenage girls who ask why they can't afford life's little extras as their friends can. I'm back to teaching again and, as you know, teachers aren't millionaires."

Her face became flushed as she said, "I want to tell them that it's their father's fault that I'm struggling to make ends meet because he just couldn't fulfill his vows to be a good husband. The girls aren't aware of the affair because I've chosen to protect them from such an unflattering portrayal of their dad. As far as they know, we're divorced just because we used to argue too much. I know I'm not supposed to feel this way, but I hate and despise him for putting me in this bind."

Coleen then revealed a struggle common to many who have suffered because of someone else's insensitivity. "I feel guilty for the fact that I'm still holding on to this tension. After all, it's been five years now, and I think I should be farther down the road toward putting this behind me." Then she sighed deeply. "Something must be really wrong with me that I am unable to forgive."

Can you relate to Coleen? Have you been haunted by problems from your past that seem insurmountable? Have you ever lectured yourself because you are not any farther down the road toward forgiveness? Have you entertained the thought that you shouldn't even be feeling the pain you feel?

Coleen's pain was legitimate and understandable. But her struggle to forgive was greatly hindered by the fact that she frequently told herself she was wrong for feeling as she did. Actually, she vacillated between allowing her emotions and scolding herself for them.

In what circumstances have you struggled to determine whether or not your pain was legitimate? (For instance, "My father was a dictator and I feared him greatly, yet now, as an adult, I feel I should be beyond my anger toward him.")

_____

_____

_____

Coming to a place of forgiveness can be a jagged process because it's easy to second-guess your memories of your experiences. Or perhaps you wonder if you are dwelling too heavily on a problem that you may have helped create. For example, shortly after her divorce a friend told Coleen, "Mark left for good reasons. Maybe he didn't break off the relationship very cleanly, but you should recall that the two of you used to argue over the smallest matters. He's not the only one who did anything wrong in your marriage."

At the time the friend spoke these words, Coleen felt very offended, as if her friend had betrayed her. Yet in the months and years following their discussion she thought, *Maybe she was right. Maybe my divorce had more to do with my faults than I care to admit.*

Think of a time you shared your pain with someone only to be told that you shouldn't feel as you did. What was said to you? (For instance, "I once told a minister about my anger toward my father, and I then received a lecture about how I was supposed to rise above my problem and become stronger because of it.")

_____

_____

_____

Coleen went back and forth saying things like, "Maybe I *am* being too hard on Mark. Even though he left me for another woman, maybe I drove him to do it." With such thoughts she would then conclude, "I don't know what to do. I don't know if I'm supposed to forgive him or if I should be the one asking for forgiveness or if I should just quit worrying about it altogether."

People like Coleen, and perhaps like yourself, should be commended when they try to factor in their own culpability regarding the breakdown of a dream. While it can be uncomfortable, it is often fair to say, "Although I have been wronged, I have also committed wrongs." It is good and noble to admit the times when your behavior has been less than ideal.

But often a problem arises as you admit your own shortcomings. You may, like Coleen, feel that your pain brought on by someone else is somehow illegitimate. Consider some of the following scenarios we have encountered in counseling as we talk with people who, like Coleen, struggle with the issue of forgiveness. Can you relate to any of these?

- Your mother had a drinking problem, causing her to neglect many of your early developmental needs. You now feel badly

4

about your past anger toward her as you realize how you, too, have struggled to be an ideal parent.

- You feel your spouse has not lived up to his or her marital vows. You've added to your already tense marriage by responding with a cynical spirit.

- Your marriage ended in divorce and your ex-partner has made unflattering and untrue statements about you. You're hurt and bitter, but you know you've done the same thing.

- Earlier in your career you were treated unfairly by a supervisor who kept you from the promotions you saw others receiving. Your work habits suffered as a result, which meant he then had the "proof" he needed to continue holding you back.

Can you understand how these vicious cycles create confusion as you try to come to terms with past wrongs? You can easily identify the improprieties others have committed, but in your quiet moments of reflection you can also see your own failings. The net result is confusion and an emotional stalemate.

Acknowledge Your Pain

Even if you can point to your own failings, you will still need permission to admit the depth of your anger or hurt or disillusionment. To do so is not a denial of your own faults. Rather, you can recognize that your feelings about someone else's mistreatment are a separate and distinct issue that deserves attention. Forgiveness can occur only as you first let yourself admit the extent of your hardship.

To help you discover whether you have legitimate struggles, check the following statements that apply to you:

— My life has been adversely impacted by someone who has had serious personal problems.

— I have had a willingness to work out interpersonal tensions, yet it has not born fruit.

— The person who wronged me knew he or she was doing wrong, but persisted anyway.

— In spite of my attempts to be reasonable, I have been faced with stubbornness or repeated wrongs.

— I feel that my good nature was clearly taken advantage of.

— My sense of trust or loyalty ultimately worked to my disadvantage.

— My desire for a fair and pleasing relationship was not matched with similar commitment or enthusiasm.

— As I look back upon the wrong behavior of another person toward me, I realize it was propelled by selfish or controlling motives.

— The misdeeds of the other person toward me could have been altered but were not.

— I have felt as if I was being treated as an inferior person.

How many items did you check? If you could respond to at least five or more of the above statements, there is a strong likelihood that you have, in fact, been on the receiving end of clearly wrong treatment. You have good reason to feel badly.

As Coleen discussed her memories and emotions with Dr. Carter, he tried to bring clarity to her situation by saying, "I can appreciate the fact that you don't just want to blame Mark for all your past marital problems while declaring yourself a completely innocent victim. To your credit, you're also trying to be fair-minded, and that's good.

"I'm concerned, though, that in your effort to be fair-minded you are going to make the task of forgiveness more difficult," he continued. "As I hear you explain your own negative contributions, you're making the mistake of fusing your problems and his problems and treating them as if they are one, which they are not. If you feel guilty for your negative contributions, then that's an issue that needs to be explored separately from the hurt you experienced when he rejected you."

Coleen then offered, "I guess I'm trying to avoid the trap that I've seen others fall into. I don't want to wallow in a victim's role by not taking responsibility for me."

"And that's appropriate for you to do," agreed the doctor. "I've known plenty of cases in which a bitter person clung so tenaciously to the victim's role that it hindered any chance for recovery. Let's agree that you'll avoid the extreme of identifying too powerfully as the victim just as you'll avoid the other extreme of not allowing yourself to truly acknowledge wrong to be wrong."

When people openly declare their pain brought on by another's failing, they often wonder: *Am I just playing some sort of blaming game?* Usually they are aware that as they describe their bad experiences, some people seem to take delight in finding fault, so this is a habit they rightly want to avoid.

Suppose for a moment that you *wanted* to portray yourself as a hapless victim of someone else's ill treatment. What sorts of thoughts might you entertain? (For instance, "I'll never be able to lead a normal life again," or "My life is completely ruined because of him.")

_____

_____

_____

By clinging too strongly to a victim status you are certain to remain stuck in a troubled way of life. You will find balance, though, when you realize you are, indeed, a victim but are not obliged to live forevermore in defeat and futility.

Now let's look at the other extreme. Suppose you are so self-effacing that you won't admit how normal your emotions might be. What might you say to yourself as a way of invalidating your painful experiences? (For instance, "I got what was coming to me," or "Maybe I directly caused the other person to act harshly toward me. It was my fault.")

Such self-blaming statements are counterproductive. They only serve to keep you stuck in a pattern of turmoil by not allowing yourself to be fully honest about what happened. So determine to be straightforward. If you were treated wrongly and were hurt it is normal, even necessary, to admit the extent of your feelings without excusing the wrongdoing.

When we counsel people like Coleen, we encourage direct discussion about the wrongful nature of what has been done. (We also discuss taking responsibility for your own faults. That issue will be explored in Chapter 11.) When we do this we encounter the question: "Isn't that just teaching people to blame and accuse?"

What do you think? In your opinion, how would you distinguish between straightforward discussion and blaming unfairly?

Unfair blame tends to be accompanied by black-and-white thinking, no gray. No room is allowed for any explanation or insight regarding the wrong deed. Straight thinking, on the other hand, will take into account the many factors involved in wrong deeds while also labeling wrong to be exactly what it is—wrong.

Dr. Carter explained to Coleen, "Even if you were a less-than-ideal wife, it does not mean that you should excuse the fact that Mark had an extended sexual liaison with another woman. Furthermore, he refused to come clean when you tried to get professional help. He did you wrong, plain and simple. That doesn't mean you and I have the right to sit in judgment over him, but it does mean that it's very understandable that you would feel betrayed and hurt, even this long after the fact."

Think about the circumstances in your past that will require forgiveness. Without being a judge, what wrongs did you unfairly have to live with? (For instance, "It was wrong that my father had such an extreme temper," or "My former boss constantly played politics as he made decisions.")

———————————————————————————————————————

———————————————————————————————————————

———————————————————————————————————————

Realize that others may not always agree with your perception of wrong. On more than a few occasions we have counseled people who were abused in some way by a parent. Upon being confronted about the past, many parents said: "You don't know what you're talking about," or "I was doing the best I knew to do." Those being counseled then feel increased stress because the perpetrators of wrong do not agree with them.

As you clearly label wrong to be wrong, keep in mind that it will rarely be met with complete agreement. Coleen told Dr. Carter, "I've had several discussions with Mark about our past problems as well as our ongoing problems. I guess I'm slow, but I'm just now realizing how skilled he is at turning the tables against me."

"I'm assuming there is a recent example you're thinking of," the doctor responded.

"Yes. Just last month I was asking him to be more considerate in the plans he makes with the girls. He has a habit of scheduling dates with them only to cancel at the last minute. But when I pointed this out to him he attacked me by saying I was so rigid I couldn't understand how plans might change. Then he went into this tirade about how it was my rigidity that brought our marriage to an end. Before I could figure it out, he had me convinced I was the bad guy."

What has someone said to you that caused you to wonder if you were the one at fault, despite evidence indicating otherwise? (For instance, "My brother has always acted aloofly and rejectingly toward me, but he says my hurt is caused by my excessive neediness.")

_____

_____

_____

In the initial steps toward forgiveness, recognize that you will be able to forgive only as you learn to overcome the tendency to discount your feelings.

Be Aware of Historical Messages Discounting Your Feelings

Usually when people like Coleen struggle to call a wrong deed wrong, they have past experiences in which their feelings or perceptions were summarily invalidated. As Coleen explored her difficulties in forgiving Mark, she admitted that her emotional responses to him were very similar to her earlier responses to her parents.

"I remember always feeling like I had to justify my feelings to my dad whenever I felt hurt or offended," she explained. "An incident stands out in which I was scolded for something my older brother had done. I was totally innocent and it caught me off guard that I was being blamed."

"So what happened when you tried to explain your position?" asked Dr. Carter.

"I never even got that far. I knew that if I opened my mouth I'd be punished double for talking back, so I just kept quiet and took the punishment."

Perhaps you can recall experiences in which you felt you had to justify feeling as you did, only to learn that your justification was not good enough. What experiences along those lines can you recall? (For instance, "My mother was a peace-at-any-cost person and I was not allowed to express anything that might stir up controversy.")

_____

_____

How did such experiences leave you feeling? (For instance, "I never felt secure about the validity of my perceptions.")

_____

_____

To get an idea of how strongly you may have been impacted by historical messages invalidating your feelings, check the following items that apply to you:

__ In my past I often felt my perceptions were not considered valid.
__ Even when I had logical explanations for my emotions they still were not accepted.
__ It was a rare day in my home when we discussed deep personal or emotional matters.
__ There were times when I just said nothing even though I felt a lot.
__ I have struggled with resentment over the fact that others couldn't understand me.
__ When I would speak my mind I got into trouble.
__ Sometimes I wonder if others consider my perspectives to be imbalanced.

__ I've told others exactly how I feel only to realize they didn't really care.

__ At times I can be hard on myself, discounting the legitimacy of my emotions.

__ Sometimes it seems that I try too hard to fit the mold others have for me.

If you checked five or more of these statements it suggests that you probably have a history of questioning your feelings. While you may have been subjected to wrong, you may feel odd in openly declaring just how hurt you feel. This is not good since it means you will probably live with too many unresolved, suppressed emotions.

Let's affirm that you are very normal to feel what you feel. Even if someone suggests that you should be responding to your problems differently, be careful that you do not automatically assume that your inner reactions are bad or wrong. No two people will ever have the same emotional response to the same set of circumstances because we differ so widely in personalities. Allow for your uniqueness. Don't assume right away that there is only one right perspective to a problem.

As Dr. Carter and Coleen discussed her long-standing tendency to accept blame for problems that were not hers, she mentioned that her dad would often punish all three kids in her family when one of them went astray. "I was constantly monitoring my brothers' behavior," she explained, "because I knew that their actions would ultimately come back on me. I felt responsible for keeping them in line."

"Can you see the parallel in the way you have handled your reactions to Mark's rejection of you?" asked Dr. Carter.

"Yeah, I can see the point you're driving home," she replied. "All my life I have taken on extra guilt, even when I'm the one who's been wronged."

"Let's tie this to your struggle to forgive. I can imagine that confusion reigns as you try to make sense of your hurt and pain. On one hand you feel like you have a legitimate claim to your hurt, but on the other hand you may tell yourself that Mark's problems are partially your fault."

She nodded as she realized how she suffered from an overdeveloped guilty conscience.

"It's not improper for you to label wrong as wrong," he continued. "It doesn't mean you will become blind to your own imperfections. It simply could mean that you are affirming the truth that you were treated poorly and you hurt because of it."

As you allow yourself to honestly label a wrong as wrong, what truth about your feelings would you be recognizing? (For instance, "I would be acknowledging that my brother's abusive behavior was clearly wrong and it was very normal that I felt fear," or "I'd be recognizing that it's normal to be frustrated because of my spouse's refusal to live according to her promises to love me.")

_____

_____

_____

Direct acknowledgment and ownership of your painful feelings are a very necessary first step in the process of forgiving. Keep in mind that you are not claiming your feelings for the purpose of accusing the wrongdoer but for the purpose of focusing on your plans for the present and future process of reconciling those emotions.

Clarify Why You Want to Forgive

Ugly truth reminds us that things go wrong, that people can and will deliberately do wrong. This is not a pleasant thought; nonetheless, we see evidences of this truth every day as we work with people in the counseling office. As you admit the extent of your hurt with no excuses or apology, you are then ready to grapple with the question: "What will I do with my pain?"

Let's underscore a very crucial thought: *You don't have to forgive.* Lest you conclude that we endorse not forgiving, let us strongly state that we believe forgiveness is right because it is part of the godly life taught and lived by Christ. We are aware, though, that your struggle to forgive may be caused by your resentment of the fact that many people tell you you *must* do so. But as you recall your hurt and pain you may have decided that forgiveness is too good of an option for the wrongdoer. Choosing to forgive will not be authentic until you first allow yourself to wrestle with the question of why you should forgive.

When have you grappled with the notion that maybe forgiveness would be letting someone else off the hook too easily? (For instance, "At times I believe a child abuser like my stepdad deserves no forgiveness," or "My ex-husband is a chronic liar and continues to create problems. Forgiveness would be too good for him.")

You are not weird for thinking such thoughts. Don't scold yourself for feeling as you do. Your first responsibility here is to be fully honest.

Coleen thought carefully as she spoke with Dr. Carter. "It feels strange for me to say it's okay that I feel deep resentment toward Mark. I'm not sure I want to say that's just the way I feel and if you don't like it, tough."

Dr. Carter smiled. "I'm not suggesting that you develop a tough-as-nails disposition since that would be so inconsistent with your temperament. I *am* saying that we need to begin with stark honesty about your pain."

Tears formed in her eyes and her bottom lip quivered. Dr. Carter was very quiet as she slowly spoke. "This is the first time in over forty years that I've been allowed to have my feelings with no requirement to hurry and get over it." She sighed deeply. "This is different."

After a moment of silence the doctor interjected, "I'm operating on a backward-sounding premise. That is, the only way to truly forgive is to permit yourself to hold on to your hurt feelings forever if that's what you want."

"But I don't want that. I want to get beyond my past."

"That's what I want for you as well, but do that with no cover-up or mandate that gives you no choice but to forgive, period."

As Coleen's right to her pain was established, she was ready to contemplate the question: Why would you choose to forgive? What's the point? As she pondered this thought Dr. Carter explained, "Ultimately forgiveness is for *your* good. You're tired of feeling angry and hurt and you may choose to move on in your life. It won't work, though, if it's purely mandatory."

Sometimes forgiveness is relatively easy because the wrongdoer expresses deep and sincere repentance and makes a genuine turnaround in his or her life. But this is not the norm. You may be struggling to forgive because the wrongdoer seems unrepentant or phony in apology. Perhaps you can accurately predict that more wrong may come from this person. This can cause you to ask the same question Coleen asked: "Why should you forgive?"

What benefit would there be to you as you choose forgiveness? (For instance, "I've got other rewarding relationships that need a whole me," or "The person most negatively impacted by my ongoing resentment is *me*.")

_____

_____

_____

Forgiveness and correcting wrong are two different issues. In some instances you may be able to insist on some form of restitution for wrong. If so, pursue it because it can greatly help the healing. But if restitution is not likely, forgiveness is still an option. You don't *have* to forgive, but you can *choose* to.

Define What Forgiveness Means to You

There are several misconceptions about what forgiveness is. We have heard many of our patients protest forgiveness for various reasons:

- "I'd just be sending the message that he (or she) can do wrong and get away with it."

- "This would mean I've got to bury my anger."

- "If I forgive it means the other person wins and I lose."

- "I guess I'll just have to put a smile on my face and say everything's all right."

- "I feel that I'm being required to go soft on something that's severely wrong."

- "One more time I've got to play the good-guy role while the bad guys just skip on their way."

Have you ever had similar thoughts? What definition of forgiveness have you entertained that made you feel that forgiveness was not a desirable quality? (For instance, "Since childhood I felt that forgiveness meant you let harsh behavior continue without declaring any boundaries.")

_____

_____

_____

How did you learn to think like that? (For instance, "My mother taught me that I'd be better off if I just dwelled on pleasant things," or "I was told not to respond to evil with evil, so I *had* to be forgiving.")

_____

_____

_____

Forgiveness can become the preferred choice only as you understand what it is and what it is not. *Forgiveness* is defined as the willingness to let go of self-harming or ineffective forms of anger, choosing instead to turn over ultimate resolution of the wrong to God.

Notice what we did not include in this definition. Forgiveness is not:

• Letting go of healthy forms of anger.

• Allowing others to continue to disrespect your needs and boundaries.

• Lying down and becoming a human doormat.

• Telling the wrongdoer that the past is no longer significant and everything's fine now.

• Agreeing to become best buddies with the wrongdoer.

• Pretending to go back to normal relations as if nothing happened.

• Denying that you may still have to live with pain caused by the wrongful deed.

Forgiveness does not always eliminate all of your pain nor does it mean that you will never feel emotions associated with the wrong that was done against you.

Forgiveness does mean:

- You will let go of the demand for repayment, particularly as you have exhausted all reasonable attempts at restitution or restoration.

- You will free yourself to focus on rewarding relationships and pursuits.

- You will choose to give up any obsessions regarding the wrongdoer, recognizing, instead, that you have better things to give your attention to.

- You will be willing to refrain from the ongoing temptation to insult the wrongdoer.

- You will let go of any illusions that you might somehow control the wrongdoer's life.

- You will be forward-looking about life, realizing that new opportunities await you.

- You will give yourself permission to make life choices that will lead to contentment and peace.

As you consider the pros and cons of forgiveness, what reasons can you find that cause you to conclude that forgiveness is a desirable choice? (For instance, "I'm ready to detach from the angry relationship with my father; I've got more important goals to pursue.")

_____

_____

_____

As Dr. Carter counseled with Coleen he explained to her, "Your choice to forgive Mark will be the beginning of several changes in the way you manage your emotions and behavior. You've been attached to Mark most of your adult life; even your anger is a form of attachment to him, so to move away emotionally from him will feel a bit strange at times."

"I never saw my not forgiving Mark as a form of attachment, but you're right," she reflected. Then smiling she said, "I really want to move forward, so it's not like I'm trying to forgive because I've *got to*. I have two daughters and lots of family and friends who need me to be a positive presence, not just a moping, depressed person tied to the past."

Can you embrace similar thoughts? Are you willing to start today on a path toward cleansing and healing? While not forgiving is a choice, forgiveness, too, is a choice, a wise choice that paves the way for a life of abundance as described in Scripture.

For instance, when Christ in His model prayer (Matt. 6:12) beseeched God to "forgive us our debts, / As we forgive our debtors," He did not add "that is, if you feel like it." His straightforward statement implied that forgiveness is a choice anchored in a broader appreciation for God's abiding forgiveness toward us.

Be honest about your pain, then be willing to choose a way of emotional management that lets you flourish. Whatever wrong you have endured, determine that you've got better plans than to let the past burden you indefinitely.

In the next two chapters we will discuss how forgiveness and healthy anger can go hand in hand. At some point, your commitment to forgive will lead you to release some of the old resentments that have plagued you. You will not be required, however, to let go of the parts of your anger that are necessary to keep you from feeling as though you are just giving up on your convictions. Balance is what we are going to help you achieve!

2

Your Legitimate Anger

Step 2. Recognize that your anger is not only normal, but necessary.

In years past we have both been privileged to speak at many conferences across America and beyond. Anytime we address emotional problems we inevitably get around to the subject of anger. The question asked more often than any other by our audiences is, "I've had moments when I *thought* that I had truly forgiven, but my anger returns from time to time. Does that mean I never really forgave the other person?"

Our guess is that you, the reader, have probably pondered similar questions. Something very unpleasant happened that caused you to feel hurt, frustrated, helpless, and angry. After many bouts with unwanted emotions you eventually came to a conscious decision that you no longer wanted to be held to the past, so you decided to forgive. Perhaps you prayed to God for healing to occur. You may actually have told the person that you would forgive him or her and tried to move forward with an improved outlook on life. But then it happened. Something reminded you of your painful experience and you struggled all over again with the hurt, the helplessness, and the anger. You tried to tell yourself that such memories and emotions should now be gone, but they persisted anyway. So you drew what seemed to be a logical conclusion: "If I still carry old emotions regarding my pain, I guess I haven't really forgiven after all."

One such person who struggled with this dilemma was Larry. Perhaps you can relate to his anguished cry: "I just can't seem to get beyond my past. I've prayed for healing many times, and I've felt like God truly heard me. I've openly voiced my commitment to forgive and have actually gone back to people who offended me and told them I no longer would hold anything against them. But there are times, particularly when I'm quiet and all alone, that my most honest thoughts remind me how I still feel cheated for what I have endured. I secretly still carry grudges."

Dr. Minirth listened carefully as Larry made this confession, sympathizing as he realized how Larry genuinely wanted to be rid of his pain. "You seem to be putting quite a lot of pressure on yourself to be completely healed of your past wounds."

"Well, at some point I have to be free from my past. The Bible says in Psalm 103:12 that when God forgives He puts the sin as far away from Himself as the east is from the west. I feel like I should too."

Larry had experienced many difficulties as a boy because of his father's alcoholism. In his teen years he had learned that his parents had a "have to" marriage because his mother had gotten pregnant out of wedlock, and Larry was the result of that pregnancy. "I always had the feeling that my dad resented me being around, so when I learned of the way they got married, it all started making sense," he explained.

During his childhood the father alternated between being aloof and being harsh. Much of the time he ignored Larry. "It's as if I didn't count," he recalled. "Many times I'd speak directly to him and he'd just keep right on doing what he was doing." Other times, the father's anger would erupt and he'd punish Larry very harshly for what seemed to be minor infractions. The anger was especially bad when his dad had been drinking.

"We never got along, and I never felt close to him," he told the doctor, "so that's why it seems so strange that I decided to go into business with him about ten years ago. No need to bore you with all the details, but it was a disaster. He treated me every bit as badly as he did when I was a boy, only this time I decided I wouldn't take it. We got into several shouting matches, and within two years we dissolved our partnership. I lost over twenty thousand dollars that he promised he'd repay. Of course, I haven't seen a dime and I never will. I can't believe I was so stupid that I thought we could work side by side."

Three years prior to his visits with Dr. Minirth, Larry had attended a weekend retreat and felt strongly moved to forgive his father for his past insensitivity. "I came to the conclusion that he didn't have a very good send-off from his family, so it was fair to assume that he didn't know any better. Besides, I was tired of the way I had become bitter and negative. In many ways I was becoming just like him. The only reasonable thing to do was to forgive him and move on. I'm a Christian, and I know God has forgiven me of much. I felt it was my duty to do the same toward my dad."

Have you ever had similar thoughts? Like Larry, have you decided that you should forgive because it was the correct thing to do? What has been your experience of forgiving only to have the old feelings of anger return? (For instance, "I forgave my brother of a serious disagreement, but every time I see him I still struggle to be friendly toward him.")

_____

_____

_____

Like Larry, do you struggle with confusion or guilt because for-giveness seems so difficult? What feelings or thoughts do you experience as this happens? (For instance, "I try to force myself to be friendly toward my brother, but it feels pretty fake.")

_____

_____

_____

Dr. Minirth explained to Larry: "Part of your tension arises from the fact that you're putting too much pressure on yourself to become something you cannot be. When you mentioned that you should put others' sins away from you as far as the east is from the west, I sensed that you felt guilty because that hasn't happened. But let's affirm something to be true: You're setting yourself up for failure if you assume that you'll be able to be as complete as God is in the forgiveness process.

"You're human, and you need to make room for that," Dr. Minirth explained. "What you have experienced hurts! And sometimes our hurts don't go away as we would like. Whereas God can completely forgive and forget, you and I stumble as we try to imitate Him."

Breathing a sigh of relief, Larry said, "When I remind myself of what you just said I wonder if I'm just trying to let myself off the hook too easily. I don't know, I just feel like I should somehow learn to get over it."

Only God can forgive and then remember the sin no more. You and I can forgive, yet still struggle with lingering memories, meaning we can still feel occasional anger. Your task, then, will be to deter-mine what to do with the lingering anger, even as you remain commit-ted to being forgiving.

As you seek balance in managing your anger toward the past, let's first get an idea of the legitimacy or normalcy of this emotion. Look over the following statements and check the ones that apply to you:

— Because of past pain I feel I need to keep my guard up more carefully than before.

— My sense of dignity was harmed, and I now want to hold more firmly to that dignity.

— I have resolved that wrong was done to me, and I need to do all that is possible to see that it is not repeated.

— Virtually anyone else who experienced what I did would probably have felt angry just as I did.

— Because of past mistreatment, I am more resolved than ever to hold on to firm convictions.

— My emotional scars remind me of how I need to be more forthright about my feelings and needs.

— I tend to be more sensitive toward others when I learn they have been subjected to difficult circumstances similar to my own.

— When I sense that the wrongdoer could still commit the same misdeeds as in the past, I wince as I recall my feelings associated with that memory.

— I now have a desire to speak out more immediately when I witness foul treatment.

— You could say that I'm not as naive or as innocent as I used to be.

Look back over these statements and recognize that they each represent a by-product of healthy anger. You will notice a consistent theme of fair play running through each statement. The more items you checked, the more it is implied that you are experiencing some normal anger.

What Is Legitimate Anger?

When trying to forgive, many people make the mistake of assuming that all anger should be removed. That is neither possible nor desirable. Bitter anger (as we will explore in the next chapter) needs to be resolved, but some anger may remain and that can be okay.

25

Before we explore the nature of legitimate anger, look into your past to determine what attitudes or beliefs you have been taught regarding the nature of anger. Have you learned that anger is bad? That Christians can't be angry because they're supposed to be always kind? That nothing good ever results from anger?

What early lessons did you receive regarding anger management? (For instance, "I was told no one wanted to hear about my bad moods," or "I assumed anger meant yelling, and that it was bad.")

_____

_____

_____

To get an indication of your level of exposure to confusing messages about anger, check the following items that apply to you:

___ As a child I was taught not to express anger because it was wrong.
___ The anger I saw in others was sufficiently negative to make me decide I'd better not let myself be the same way.
___ I think I was overtaught the values of kindness and forgiveness because I've not permitted myself to admit how angry I really can be.
___ There are times when my people-pleasing tendencies dictate my relating style.
___ If I feel angry about a problem that no longer exists, I feel as if I should hurry up and get over it.
___ When I sense that others no longer want to hear about my past problems I may clam up.
___ I can't seem to get over my anger if the offending person remains unrepentant, though I assume I should.
___ As I think about my suffering I remind myself that others have suffered as badly or worse, so I ought to count my blessings.
___ I assume that once anger is resolved that means it should be out of my system.

— I just don't want to be known as an angry person, so I pressure myself to act composed.

Go back over the statements and recognize how each item implies that anger should be neatly tied and finished. How many did you check? If you checked five or more, there is a strong likelihood that you feel confused about the normalcy or legitimacy of this emotion. As a result, you will probably struggle to feel right about your efforts to forgive if there is any lingering anger.

Let's affirm that forgiveness can occur even if you still carry some aftereffects of anger. If your anger has understandable roots and if you are not using your anger to justify ongoing harsh or disruptive behavior, you can be considered normal.

Anger can be best understood as you realize it is linked to your sense of self-preservation. Think about moments when you feel angry. (By the way, in speaking of anger we include episodes of frustration, annoyance, irritability, impatience, and disgust.) What provokes the emotion? Inevitably you feel slighted, ignored, misunderstood, invalidated, or disrespected. Perhaps you may not always manage the resulting emotion correctly, but as you examine the roots of your anger, it is almost always sparked by your instinct to protect yourself or to preserve what you believe to be right.

Anger, then, can be defined as the emotion of self-preservation that enables you to stand up for your worth, your needs, or your convictions. Through anger you are wishing to communicate: "Hey, show me some respect, won't you?" Or, "You've violated a conviction of mine, and I don't like it."

Dr. Minirth explained to Larry, "The fact that you still experience anger can be explained by the presence of solid convictions that have been violated. Without condemning your father, we can realize that he did not live up to the role God intended for him as a husband or dad. Neither did he follow business practices that are necessary for a thriving enterprise. Though you have chosen to let go of any effort to seek retribution, the memory of his violations can still stir up your convictions."

How about you? As you experience ongoing anger because of past foul treatment, what convictions are you preserving? (For instance, "I still think about my ex-wife's infidelity, and it reminds me how necessary sexual purity is to a marriage.")

_____

_____

_____

What is good about your convictions that are a part of your anger? (For instance, "More than ever I am resolved to treat people in ways I wish I had been treated.")

_____

_____

_____

Larry was weary of holding bitterness toward his father, but in his desire to be forgiving he had assumed that any struggle with his emotions meant he had failed. He was utilizing an all-or-nothing thinking style that was unrealistic. "I had always assumed," he admitted, "that the only way to root out my anger was to get rid of all of it. It never dawned on me that some of the emotion was okay."

In order to more fully recognize why our anger is normal, let's take a look at four factors that commonly accompany bitter or hurt responses.

1. You Hoped for Some Form of Intimacy or Favored Treatment

Few people linger long in their hurt when the offending person is someone of minor stature or fleeting importance. For instance, if you hear of a Hollywood star who has an extramarital affair, the news is brushed off as common gossip. But if it is *your* spouse who has an affair, you are devastated. What's the difference? It's simple. You expected intimacy or special treatment from your spouse in a way that stands separate from your expectations regarding others.

Even if the offending party is someone you had virtually no ties to (for instance, if you were the victim of a random criminal act), your hurt stems from an assumption that people should treat fellow humans with decency. This desire is in each of us, and it is quite normal.

Dr. Minirth asked Larry to talk about the hopes he once held regarding his relationship with his father. Larry responded, "I remember as a boy that I would see how my friends' dads treated them. I was amazed that some of them seemed to share a friendship with their fathers. I really envied that because I could not recall one single warm moment my dad and I shared."

"You realize how normal it was for you to hope for that kind of father/son closeness, don't you?"

"Well, sometimes I wondered what *normal* really was," Larry said, "but yes, I feel like my dad could have at least made an effort. I wouldn't have required perfection, just an effort."

"Let's go farther with this thought," Dr. Minirth said. "Do you ever recall feeling hopeful or optimistic that just maybe you and your dad could somehow overcome your differences?"

He nodded. "Several years ago when my dad and I tried going into business together, I addressed some of my concerns very openly with him. He seemed to hear me, and I felt we had a pretty decent respect for each other, particularly in comparison to our past intolerance."

"So you got just a taste of closeness, and it caused you to hope for more."

"That's right. But, boy, was I taken for a ride! When we hit our first major disagreement, out came his angry and controlling nature, just like before, and it was downhill from there."

Perhaps you, like Larry, can recall how hopes for a favored relationship were severely dashed. Perhaps you had the disheartening experience of realizing that the ones you loved were only using you. Perhaps someone who seemed to have much to offer also was very overbearing and insensitive. Some of the more common disappointments we have encountered in our counseling include:

- Children who looked to adult family members and older siblings for protection, only to become the victims of abuse or foul treatment.

- Marriage partners whose romantic hopes were dashed through years of conflict.

- Siblings who looked to one another for family support, only to be manipulated or rejected.

- Business partners whose aspirations for success were laid low by financial improprieties.

- Christian friends who opened their hearts in hopes of finding loving support, only to be judged.

What hopes have you had for favored treatment or intimate belonging? (For instance, "When I married I assumed my mate would be fully trustworthy," or "I truly believe it is normal to want my father to be proud of me simply because I am his son.")

_____

_____

_____

What happened to those hopes that have caused emotional struggles? (For instance, "My friend that I trusted explicitly told other people about very confidential facts," or "My willingness to be loyal was taken as an excuse to manipulate me.")

Can you understand how your feelings of hurt or anger are predictable? When you open your life to another you naturally hope that decency will result. Even as you determine to forgive you are not required to deny those emotions.

2. You Felt Betrayed

Perhaps the frustration we most commonly hear among people struggling to forgive is: "I feel so betrayed and so violated." Whether the angry person was abused by a relative or jilted by a lover or backstabbed by a friend, the common cry is: "How could you *do* this to me?"

What is it that makes betrayal so difficult to accept?

When you feel betrayed it is because of a violated trust. Most of the time the offending person gave the appearance of being someone who could be trusted. But that trustworthiness proved to be false, phony.

Larry told Dr. Minirth, "One thing always confused me about my father. When I saw him in public he could be the nicest guy around. He knew many people by name. He could tell a good story, ask about the things that interested others, laugh easily. I was amazed at the way he could work a crowd. I remember wishing I could be as socially skilled as he was.

"But when he was at home it was like Dr. Jekyll turning into Mr. Hyde. He was grumpy and forever in a foul mood. I'd wonder what was so awful about me that caused his switch to flip."

"So your father was a master at portraying an image when it suited his purpose," Dr. Minirth reflected, "but the *real* person was what you saw."

31

"I guess that describes it well, at least as I understand it now. But back then I didn't realize that his happy-go-lucky act was just a show. I really thought his rejection of me had something to do with my deficiencies. I kept trying to adjust to his requirements until I finally learned as an adult that I'd never satisfy him. Then I began wondering why he even bothered being a dad at all. Why would he take on a wife and kids if he had no willingness to live up to the role?"

Can you see how Larry's bitterness was tied to his disillusionment caused by the hope that his father would be trustworthy? That's betrayal.

What image did your offending person present to you as you initially came to know him or her? (For instance, "My mate led me to believe he would always be a supportive presence," or "My mother was pleasant to outsiders, which led me to assume she'd be pleasant to me.")

_____

_____

_____

What happened that made you feel duped or betrayed? (For instance, "I learned my parents never really wanted me," or "My business partner was broke and left me to pay his debts.")

_____

_____

_____

Are you wrong or foolish to hope for trustworthiness in others? No, not really. Interdependence is part of life. The Bible speaks often about interchanges with others that imply that one's quality of life will be enhanced because of them:

• Bear one another's burdens (Gal. 6:2).

• Love one another (John 13:34).

- Encourage and stimulate one another (Heb. 10:24–25).

- Be kind to one another (Eph. 4:32).

- Regard one another as more important than yourself (Phil. 2:3).

God's perfect design calls for humans to be there for one another, to challenge one another, and to uphold one another. By hoping for a connection with someone significant you are merely attempting to live within that design. You are not to be faulted for doing so nor are you to be faulted for feeling disillusioned because someone else chose not to respect that design. Your feeling of betrayal implies that you genuinely believe in the correctness of injecting respect and responsibility into interpersonal actions.

What *right* convictions lie behind your feelings of betrayal? (For instance, "It's right to believe others should keep confidentiality," or "It's right to believe family members should be respectful to one another.")

_____

_____

_____

3. The Betrayal Had Moral Overtones

Nearly every act of betrayal is connected to matters of right versus wrong. In fact when morality is not involved in an act, we are not likely to feel the pain that requires forgiveness. Consider, for instance, that a coworker has been promoted ahead of you for a position you aspired to obtain. Do you feel any emotion? Yes, most likely you will feel envy. Because the promotion was gained through fair means, though, betrayal is not an issue. But let's suppose you later learned that this coworker cheated to get ahead of you and also lied about his qualifications for the position. Now what emotion do you feel?

Betrayal. Because you've been passed over as a result of this person's immorality, your pain is deeper.

Although we live in an era when people seem to wink glibly at immorality, at the core of our humanness we still realize that morality matters. Somewhere inside we cling to the belief that relationships can be fulfilling only as we subscribe to basic precepts of right and wrong. In fact, it is our anger at injustice that can cause us to become crusaders for what is right. This is why we caution our patients not to let go of anger completely. Without anger, we may demonstrate little or no concern for morals.

As Dr. Minirth and Larry discussed the normalcy of his lingering anger, Larry reflected, "It never dawned on me until you mentioned it that my anger is my way of staying in touch with my convictions of right and wrong. But I can see it clearly now in nearly every angry experience I've had."

"Many times people display their anger ineffectively," the doctor explained, "so we assume that nothing good is associated with the emotion. But if you consider your moments of deepest frustration, you hurt because you don't want to let go of your convictions. There's something good to be said for that."

"When I was a boy," Larry recalled, "it used to bother me that Dad had to numb out with his alcohol. I saw how it transformed his personality into something very distasteful, something very harmful. Even at a young age I knew Dad could choose not to be harsh, and the fact that he chose to be mean-spirited told me that he didn't care. Right and wrong didn't matter to him, but it did to me."

"You've chosen to forgive your dad, which is the right thing to do, but let's look at this further," said Dr. Minirth. "In forgiving him, do you also want to cease believing in your morals?"

"Well, of course not," came the reply. "More than ever I want to be *known* for those morals."

"Then you won't be able to remove all of your anger," said Dr. Minirth. "Your emotion represents your ongoing commitment to what you believe. That commitment does not need to become an excuse for rowdy or condemning anger, but it *can* still arouse your feelings."

How about you? You've chosen to forgive, but will you also choose to disengage from your moral foundations? As you consider the wrongs you have suffered, what morality was violated? (For instance, "My sister finds it too convenient to tell lies," or "My father divorced my mother because he put his sexual desires ahead of his commitment to his family.")

_____

_____

_____

Why were you right to feel hurt or angry? (For instance, "My anger represented my commitment to truth.")

_____

_____

_____

Your desire for vengeance may need to be removed. Perhaps you will even need to accept the fact that wrongdoers may go unpunished. Forgiveness will help you in such instances. But your forgiveness will not require you to let go of your values. Hold on to them. Yes, you may need to monitor the intensity of the emotion accompanying those values, but let's not throw morality away.

4. You Continue to Feel Bereavement

Following your experience of pain, you will continue to experience ongoing stress because of the bereavement it creates. Divorcees will need to learn to forgive their ex-spouses, yet they will forever have to live with the feelings of loss regarding the broken marriage. Abuse survivors will need to put their painful pasts to rest, yet the feeling of lost innocence will linger for years. Victims of crime will need to lay aside bitterness or hate, yet this does not mean they should ignore their loss of trust.

Our point is that when you have suffered wrongdoing, your feelings of loss will linger long after the wrong act itself. You will experience reminders of what might have been. Emptiness or struggle will not quickly go away. Forgiveness does not always remove all grief.

Larry explained to Dr. Minirth, "Three years ago at that conference I realized I needed to let go of the bitterness that my past put inside me. But you know my hardest struggle? Financially I'm still trying to get out from under debt because of my failed business with my dad. I can't own a home; I rent because I can't afford a down payment. Every month is tight at our house and I cringe when my wife complains about simple things we can't buy. I don't blame her for wanting a little financial freedom; she's not a greedy person. But I'm behind because of what my dad did."

Can you recognize the feeling of loss Larry was experiencing? Though he had decided that he wanted to let go of his bitterness toward his father, he could not completely avoid the ongoing repercussions of the problems they had shared. Can you relate to this?

What loss have you experienced as a result of being wronged? (For instance, "Since my divorce I have lost the respect of people who judge me," or "My strained relationship with my sister causes me to have less camaraderie with the rest of my extended family.")

_____

_____

_____

What emotions do you feel as a result of your loss? (For instance, "The loss of my marriage causes me to feel lonely," or "My rift with the extended family makes me feel discouraged.")

_____

_____

_____

A goal of forgiveness can be the minimizing of those emotions associated with your loss. But it would be unrealistic to say that forgiveness completely cures *all* painful emotions.

Dispelling the Myth

People like Larry who assume that they should cease to struggle with undesirable emotions are living with the mythical notion that forgiveness means the past should no longer evoke tension. They assume that their natural human reactions to pain should somehow cease.

Dr. Minirth explained, "The greatest act of forgiveness was demonstrated by Jesus as He spoke His words of forgiveness on the cross. Specifically He forgave the ones who were responsible for hanging Him there, but He was also demonstrating His enormous capacity for love." Larry nodded as Dr. Minirth continued. "But I want you to ponder this question: Does the Bible indicate that God forever after ceases having painful reactions to sin?"

Larry realized where Dr. Minirth was going in his reasoning. The doctor continued. "Even after Christ's triumphal resurrection, Ephesians 4:30 makes it clear that God is still grieved and saddened by sin. In the same way, your choice to forgive will not eliminate all other emotions."

Forgiveness does not require you to feel healed of all emotions at all times. Forgiveness implies you are committed to the *process* of healing. You may still feel aftereffects of your wounds, yet in your willingness to forgive you can choose not to exaggerate your reactions to those feelings.

Consider the following illustrations of this idea:

- A woman feels uneasy as relatives discuss matters regarding her father with whom she has an estranged relationship. Rather than feeding her pain by insisting they should immediately cease talking about him, she lets the conversation continue while giving herself permission not to feel as they do toward him.

- A father talks with his adult son who has been a severe disappointment because of past manipulation and disrespect. He hurts inwardly as he is reminded of the turmoil the son created, yet he freely chooses to be civil in their discussion.

- A social acquaintance is unaware that a woman's husband has committed adultery, so she speaks glowing words about how reliable he is. The wife is painfully reminded of the severe problems he has created, yet she does not feel it is necessary to correct the acquaintance's impressions.

In each of these illustrations a residual emotion is experienced by the person who has chosen to forgive, yet there is also a desire to remain committed to the *process* of healing. Most people who have suffered deep loss will admit that the healing may never be complete, yet forgiveness is the path they choose.

What implications does this idea have for you? Even as you feel ongoing emotions associated with your loss, how can you also show your commitment to the process of healing? (For instance, "Though I am reminded of my feelings of betrayal each time my former business partner is mentioned, I have concluded that I have better things to do than police his activities.")

In this chapter we have explored how the path toward forgiveness allows you to be honest about the inevitable emotions that linger for a long time after you've decided to forgive. In the next chapter we will explore how to keep those emotions from turning into perpetual bitterness or resentment.

3

Uprooting Bitterness

Step 3. Realize how ongoing bitterness will ultimately hurt you.

Several months passed after Larry's consultations with Dr. Minirth. He had recommitted himself to forgiving his father for their past broken relations and had determined that he would just let bygones be bygones. But . . .

During the Thanksgiving season Larry and his family traveled several hours to stay a few nights in his hometown with his sister. The visit was especially pleasant because he and Elizabeth shared a very close relationship. Their spouses got along fine with each other and the kids, as usual, enjoyed spending time with their cousins. Holidays with his little sister were a true joy.

On the second day of the visit Elizabeth received a phone call. It was Dad. He was bored, had time on his hands, so he'd stop by to see the grandkids, he said. Elizabeth wasn't sure what to say to Larry, knowing he wouldn't be pleased. But before she could speak, Larry said, "That was Dad on the phone, wasn't it?" Then remembering his determination to forgive he said, "I'm not going to let him get under my skin. If he wants to come over, I'll handle it just fine. I'm determined not to get pulled down by our past." Famous last words.

The visit went terribly. Though Dad swore he hadn't been drinking, Larry smelled the bourbon on his breath as soon as they met, and that set the stage for Larry. Immediately he recalled holidays from his childhood that were ruined because Dad had gone on drinking binges. In the old days when he drank there was nothing good that came from him. He was loud and obnoxious, and, while he was always ready with a funny story during those times, he was also prone to angry outbursts that would send Larry and Elizabeth into hiding. As a boy, Larry hated holidays since they were so predictably unpredictable. Now, here was the grandfather who wanted to play the good-guy role with his family, but Larry knew better.

When Dad greeted the five grandkids they were somewhat indifferent to him. After the initial hugs the kids quickly found other things to do, and Dad's feelings were hurt. "What's their problem?" he growled. "Don't they have any respect for their grandfather?" He tried to engage the kids in play, but his lack of sincerity and warmth kept the children at bay. Simply put, they did not connect. But that was nothing new. They had never connected with their grandfather.

"I'll tell you young folks a thing or two," he bellowed to Larry and Elizabeth. "When I was their age I was taught to respect my elders. This generation is filled with a bunch of spoiled brats who don't understand the meaning of the word *respect.*"

Elizabeth tried playing peacekeeper, "Now, Daddy, don't get upset. They're just kids, and you know how easily distracted they can be. They don't mean any harm."

Determined to be in a bad mood, Dad replied, "I don't care if they mean harm or not. They could still have a few manners. Did it ever occur to you that it's your job to teach them to act properly?"

Larry interrupted. "Dad, let's not get into any problems right now.

We don't get to spend much time together as it is, so let's just lighten up and have a relaxing visit."

"Maybe you should lighten up, Mr. Know-it-all. Who asked your opinion anyway?"

"You've been drinking today, haven't you, Dad? That's what this is all about, isn't it? Just like it was thirty years ago, you go straight to the bottle during the holidays, and you make life miserable for everyone else. You'll never change!"

By now Elizabeth was really rattled. "Larry, let's drop the subject. We don't need the tension."

Dad chimed in, "No, let's not drop the subject. Mr. High-and-mighty here seems to have a problem with his old man, and I'd like to know more about it."

You can imagine how the scene went from there. It was downhill all the way.

After the holiday, Larry was back in Dr. Minirth's office. "I know you told me that it's normal to have ongoing emotions even after I've decided to forgive," he explained, "but I'm worried that I'm going to become so bitter that I'll lose my emotional balance."

"You're on track with your thinking," the doctor assured him. "Balance is what we're looking for, but you need permission to be human. I don't think your recent frustration with your dad was out of the ordinary, but you are wise to consider how to keep bitterness from setting in."

"I was reading a Bible passage recently and came across Ephesians 4:31, which says to put away bitterness and wrath and clamor," Larry said. "Then the next verse instructs us to be kind and tender-hearted and forgiving. If I let bitterness grab hold of me, I'll lose my ability to forgive."

Larry was right. Bitterness can erase the effectiveness of your choice to forgive. Can you relate to his plight?

When are you most susceptible to bitterness? (For instance, "My mother refuses to let me be an adult, and I dread her visits," or

"I feel embittered as I see my spouse being friendly to the public but not to me.")

_____

_____

_____

It's okay, even necessary, to admit that you struggle with bitterness. You won't be able to get beyond its grip unless you can admit its presence. To get an idea of the extent of your bitterness, check the following items that often apply to you:

__ It bothers me when I see that the wrongdoer seems to be progressing with a normal life.

__ I wish my feelings and boundaries would be more openly respected by the one who did me wrong.

__ Reminders of my past pain and frustration seem to come at me too frequently and intensely.

__ It bothers me when others don't realize the extent of my anguish.

__ I struggle with the feeling that life is not fair.

__ Compared to others, I seem to be lagging behind in my efforts to live a contented life.

__ I still feel controlled by my past problems. They just don't seem to go away.

__ I am more subdued and withdrawn than I used to be, and I don't like it.

__ Others seem to expect me to just shake off my past problems and move on.

__ There are times when I still yearn for vengeance against the person who wronged me.

Don't be surprised if you checked several of these items. The greater your pain, the greater your struggle will be to fight off the feelings associated with it. If you checked more than five items, you're susceptible to bitter feelings. By no means does this indicate that you are abnormal. It simply means that your path to recovery will be less than perfectly smooth. But you can get there!

Dr. Minirth spoke kindly to Larry. "I know you feel that you're stuck in your old patterns, but you need not give up on yourself. Forgiveness would be easy if the one you are forgiving was totally repentant and sorrowful. But with your dad that doesn't seem to be the case, at least not for now. Let's look at ways to keep your bitterness from becoming a stronghold in your life."

See Bitterness as an Option

"A major mistake made by people attempting to forgive," explained Dr. Minirth, "is that they tell themselves that they absolutely cannot let themselves feel this way. But when they do this they make their struggle with bitterness *more* intense."

At first glance, it may seem strange that we would suggest that bitterness is an option. After all, the goal is to become free from bitterness, isn't it? As you consider this concept, realize that it is your approach to emotional management we want you to examine. Do you handle your emotions with dutiful mandates or with choices?

A common ingredient in a healthy personality is freedom to choose. Ultimately, no one likes to live within a system that is so regimented that options cease to exist. This is true in the world of work, in marriages, in extended family relations, and it is true in the realm of emotional management. To operate at peak performance, you need to know you can choose what direction you will go.

Consider for a moment how you have learned to respond to undesired emotions such as hate or resentment or disgust. In the past when you have exposed these feelings, what types of responses did you hear from others? Did others tend to respond with understanding? With words of comfort? With curiosity? If your experience is like most people's, you can recall many times when your negative emotions were met with an instruction to feel otherwise.

For example, Larry recalled talking with his sister, Elizabeth, about his struggle to forgive their dad. As he exposed his recurring feelings of bitterness she responded with, "You're just going to have to learn not to expect anything from him. That way you won't get hurt."

"How did her response make you feel?" asked the doctor.

"Well, I know Elizabeth meant well. She's a sweet woman, but when she told me that, I could immediately feel myself shutting down."

"Like you didn't want to risk offending her?"

"Exactly. My sister knows how hardheaded and condescending Dad can be," Larry explained. "Yet she doesn't realize how betrayed I really felt by the way he enticed me into business with him only to pull the rug out from under me."

Have you had any experiences similar to Larry's? When have you risked exposing your bitterness only to have someone tell you what to do with it? (For instance, "I can't tell my husband how disappointed I feel about my extended family because he will tell me to just get over it.")

_____

_____

_____

When you are reminded that you shouldn't feel as you do, what effect does this have on you? (For instance, "My bitterness actually becomes stronger; but then I fear that my feelings will be exposed, so I hide what I feel.")

_____

_____

_____

What would you prefer instead? (For instance, "I'd like to have permission to feel as I do, with the understanding that I'll not remain stuck in my lousy emotions forever.")

_____

_____

_____

Most people trying to make sense of their emotions want the freedom to feel them openly and honestly. When this is allowed, their ability to apply choices and gain perspective increases.

Dr. Minirth explained to Larry, "It may be that Elizabeth will never fully be able to empathize with your moods, but at least *you* can do yourself a big favor."

Larry was listening carefully.

"Give yourself the permission to feel what you feel, even if it may not be what you want to feel."

Larry's eyes opened wide. "Are you telling me to go ahead and stay bitter? What if I tell myself to hold on to my anger and it just doesn't go away?"

Dr. Minirth smiled calmly. "That's a risk we're taking, isn't it?

"Let me explain why I think it's necessary first to consider bitterness as an option. People tend to respond poorly when required to live strictly according to mandates. If your only reason for dropping bitterness is that you *have* to, you'll not remain committed to your decision over the long course. You need to know that your directions are freely chosen, which means that you acknowledge the bad options as well as the good ones."

In order for you to allow yourself to consider bitterness as an option, what would have to change in your thinking? (For instance, "I guess I'd be forced to drop some of my all-or-nothing thinking," or "I'd have to be less legalistic in my thinking and more realistic.")

_____

_____

_____

Explore the Consequences of Bitterness

By allowing bitterness to be an option, we are not endorsing it as the preferred emotion. In fact, we have each seen productive lives destroyed by bitterness, and we realize that it can have long-lasting effects on you and those connected to you.

What we are saying is this: The freedom to choose bitterness can then cause you to ask yourself penetrating questions. You will be more inclined to ask: "Who am I? Why would I choose bitterness over forgiveness? What is the likely outcome of my choices, either for bitterness or for forgiveness?"

Larry considered Dr. Minirth's words carefully. "I guess I've always tried to make choices correctly mainly because I didn't want to do something against my Christian principles. But really, I *have* been issuing myself mandates."

"And the result?"

"The mandates don't work. They just make me feel guilty for being me."

"I happen to believe that bitterness will cause more harm than good," explained Dr. Minirth, "so I don't mind admitting that I'm biased. I'd like to see you put it away, just as the Bible describes in Ephesians 4:31. But before you can claim ownership to your choice to forgive, you'll need to grapple with the question of why. I'm confident that you'll arrive at the conclusion that you *want* to let go of your bitterness."

Let's examine a few questions here for the purpose of personalizing your choice to drop bitterness.

First, be honest and ask yourself, "Why would I want to remain bitter?" (For instance, "It makes me feel powerful," or "I can't imagine myself feeling happy again," or "It gives me the excuse I need to withdraw.")

_____

_____
_____

Now ask, "What would be the likely consequences of clinging to bitterness?" (For instance, "I'd be less effective in developing love relationships," or "It could become a habit that would eat away at my quality of life.")

_____

_____

_____

In our years of counseling people for depression, anger, anxiety, and the like, we have *never* encountered anyone who ultimately experienced pleasant consequences from holding on to bitterness. It is doubtful that you will find the consequences of bitterness to be good either.

Realizing that bitterness is a choice but its consequences are not desirable, you should be willing to move on to further questions.

How would you benefit by choosing to set aside bitterness? (For instance, "Perhaps I'd be less critical in general," or "I'd cease letting someone else pull my emotional strings.")

_____

_____

_____

Why might forgiveness be a better option than bitterness? (For instance, "I'd be choosing not to live in the past, which would free me to be more effective in my current relationships," or "I could concentrate more on qualities that I *do* want to have in my personality.")

_____

_____

_____

What consequences might you expect by choosing forgiveness? (For instance, "I'd have a clean conscience," or "I'd have more energy to pursue normal activities.")

_____

_____

_____

You are not duty-bound to forgive nor are you duty-bound to cease your bitterness. On numerous occasions we have worked with people who have been intent on proving that they can be as bitter and depressed as anyone alive, and no one can stop them. While we believe that such determination is ultimately futile, we are also aware that no amount of coercion could *make* those people choose otherwise. People are free to choose, even if it means they might make poor choices.

Our hope is that you will see the wisdom in laying your bitterness down, not because you are required to but because this is the most beneficial of all your options.

Choose Between Bondage and Liberation

As you explore the options involved in managing bitterness, consider how you feel about being held in a life of bondage. That's what bitterness ultimately is. By clinging to your resentments, you are being held captive by the person who has wronged you, sometimes for years after the fact.

Dr. Minirth explained this to Larry. "As you talk about your feelings toward your dad, get a mental picture of a rope with one end tied around your waist and the other tied around his. You are unable to move forward successfully because you are dragging his weight with you wherever you go. Furthermore, you are susceptible to being yanked off your path when he chooses to move in directions counter to your goals."

"Wow! I've never really thought of it like that, but that pretty clearly describes how it is."

"You can complain about the discomfort that rope creates, especially when you are pulling against each other, and you can wish aloud that he'd change his direction to parallel yours." Larry nodded as the doctor spoke. "But ultimately, you can decide if you want to allow the rope to remain tied around your waist. *He* doesn't have to untie himself for you to be free. You have the choice to do it on your own."

In what ways has your bitterness caused you to feel enslaved? (For instance, "I can't move forward in my new love relationship because I'm still fuming about my ex-spouse's poor treatment of me.")

_____

_____

_____

How have you contributed to the feeling of bondage this brings? (For instance, "I'm so preoccupied thinking about the frustrations created by the other person that I don't pursue my own freely chosen path.")

_____

_____

_____

Dr. Minirth explained to Larry, "When you were a boy your emotions were indeed tied to the behaviors of your parents. You were dependent upon them to the extent that they would directly determine your quality of life. I guess we could say that your tender age and incomplete thinking skills bound you to them whether you wanted it to be that way or not."

Larry nodded as he recalled scenes from his childhood when he felt paralyzed by his dad's harsh ways. He distinctly remembered feeling stuck because he was so uncomfortable with his father's inconsistencies while realizing he had no place to go for real relief.

"The good news is that you are now an adult, and you have the ability to think and choose your own separate path. But unfortunately, your emotional responses sometimes still resemble those of a young boy who feels tied to his parents."

"So, in a kind way," said Larry, "you're suggesting that I free myself from his control."

"That's right. As a kid you weren't capable of removing yourself from him, but as an adult you are no longer in bondage."

If you, like Larry, were to choose to drop the shackles of bondage to persons who have failed you, what would have to change in your approach toward them? (For instance, "I'd quit trying to figure out the motives behind my ex-husband's every move," or "I'd remind myself that my former boss is not God, though he tries to act like it.")

In the days of slavery, slaves were not set free until given papers by their owners declaring them free. But you are not such a slave! You don't have to wait for a human to give you freedom papers. God Himself created you with a free will. If a human cannot recognize your legitimate needs, if a human prefers to treat you in a manner of bondage, that never negates your freedom. You are in bondage to no human.

Larry thought carefully about this idea. "So you're saying that I became enslaved to my dad as soon as I entertained the possibility that we might have a decent holiday visit?" He paused. "I'm thinking of a couple of adjustments I could make. First, I need to give myself permission not to see him if that's what it takes to remain bitter-free. Second, when I am around him I need to drop my expectation that he'll be anything other than what he is."

How about you? What adjustments could you make to unchain yourself from someone who has let you down? (For instance, "I need to quit seeking out gossip regarding my ex-spouse," or "I'm giving up the hope that my brother will ever be pleasant to me.")

Release Justice to God

When was the first time you became aware of justice, that wrongs should be corrected with some form of punishment or retribution? You were probably a very young child. If you hit your sister there were consequences to pay once your parents caught you. If you cheated at school you would receive a zero. If you were caught cutting in the lunch line, you were sent to the end of the line. You get the picture. The concept of justice has been reinforced throughout your life.

A major roadblock to forgiveness is the requirement that justice must first be served. Because we each learned early in life that wrong must be repaid, we carry a logical sense of justice with us throughout our adult years. If a close friend has failed you, for instance, you want some acknowledgment that wrong was done, and you want a show of repentance. If you determine that a parent gave you an improper upbringing, you'd like some form of apology and change. If a spouse failed you, you'd like consequences to be forthcoming so the impropriety will not be repeated.

Inwardly you can cling to the notion that fairness should always win over injustice. And as logical as it may seem to hope for that, you can set yourself up for bitterness when you face the possibility that justice may never be served.

That was Larry's dilemma as he struggled to come to terms with his father's difficult personality. "I'd like to hear him say *just once* that he knew he'd done me wrong," Larry told Dr. Minirth. "All my life he's been hard-edged and cross. He's a selfish user who cares little about the needs and feelings of those closest to him. And plenty of people have felt pain because of his gross insensitivity." Then shaking his head he said, "It seems that everyone but *him* has felt pain. He's the one in our family who's brought misery to the table, but he seems to just waltz away from the hurt unscathed and no worse for the wear."

"Not at all fair, is it?" the doctor sympathized.

"No, it isn't! That's what eats away at me. When I try to forgive him I keep getting pulled back into bitterness by the unfairness of it all."

Do you ever feel this way? As you consider your struggle with the one who has wronged you, what unfairness do you encounter? (For instance, "Not only did my husband leave me for another woman, but he's doing fine financially while I'm the one struggling to make ends meet.")

What have you attempted to do to see that fairness is achieved? (For instance, "I've asked my closest friends to have no contact with my ex-husband," or "I tried to confront my mother constructively about changes she could make.")

Unfortunately, if your experience is like many others', you may have learned that in some cases no amount of effort can guarantee justice. Many wrongdoers seemingly have a knack for defying accountability. Some have insufficient guilt or remorse regarding their misdeeds. Some even have no awareness at all that they have done anything wrong.

What can you do when justice seems nonexistent?

Inherent in our definition of forgiveness is the willingness to leave ultimate justice to God. Forgiveness does *not* require you to suppress

54

your feelings, to shrug at the wrongs dealt to you, or to become allies with your antagonist. But forgiveness *does* require that you hand over the ultimate consequences of another's wrongdoing to God.

We find that releasing justice to God is difficult for two reasons:

1. God does not always work in ways we can see or understand.
2. Yielding to God forces us to admit exactly how limited, even powerless, we are.

As you consider the process of letting God manage justice, what mysteries or uncertainties block your efforts? (For instance, "I don't like waiting on God's timetable; it seems slow," or "Sometimes I doubt that God even hears my prayers.")

_____

_____

_____

No one likes admitting the extent of his or her powerlessness. When you realize how limited you are in exacting justice, what protests run through your mind? (For instance, "I'm tired of having to be the one who always takes the moral high road," or "I hate to think the wrongdoer is allowed to feel that he's better than me.")

_____

_____

As we counsel patients struggling to forgive, we encourage them with the notion that tremendous freedom and relief can be found as they let go of their pain long enough to let God be God. By stepping away from the effort to force justice upon an unrepentant person you can expend your emotional energy on more satisfying pursuits, focusing on things that can be rewarding to you.

But first, let's be honest about your limits. Be willing to admit what you simply cannot do. For instance:

55

- You cannot force another person to be aware of your feelings.

- You cannot make an individual accept responsibility for wrong-doing.

- You can share your needs with God, but then you have to recognize that you cannot dictate anything to Him. After all, He's God and you are not.

- You are limited in your ability to apply consequences that might cause the wrongdoer to think about his or her actions.

- You are limited in your ability to sway others' opinions so they will support your needs and views.

- Your communication capabilities are limited. They hinge on the willingness of others to hear and absorb.

People who cannot seem to forgive harm themselves because they cannot accept the reality of limits. Their bitterness implies that they wish they could possess God-like powers that they will never have.

You can make major progress, though, when you choose to accept your limits. For instance, Larry admitted to Dr. Minirth, "I can see in retrospect that I lost my ability to forgive when I assumed that I could talk with Dad about his drinking habits in a way that would cause him to come to terms with the harm it creates." Shaking his head he added, "It's hard for me to accept that he doesn't give a flip about my opinions. Intellectually, I know I'm talking to a brick wall, but emotionally I don't want to live with the reality that I can't change him."

"At the time you encountered your dad you were in a good mood and you were hoping you could talk him into being in one too," Dr. Minirth reflected. "But I guess you're going to have to get used to the fact that no amount of persuasion will change him."

Larry's eyes brightened. "If I can remember that, I won't get pulled into my foul moods as easily. I'd like nothing more than to say, "Okay, God, this is where You take over. I'll let You handle Dad's drinking problem because I can't.""

If you chose to accept your limits, letting God be in charge of your antagonist, what would be the result? (For instance, "I'd quit chasing down every rumor my ex-spouse states about me and stand on my own good character," or "I wouldn't talk so harshly to family and friends about my past problems with my brother. I'd dwell on happier subjects.)

_____

_____

_____

By living within your limits you will be free to focus on what can be good in your life rather than spinning your wheels struggling against the things that cannot be changed.

Apply Your Efforts in Small Increments of Time

In an attempt to ease Larry's potential pressures, Dr. Minirth said, "I'm aware that the things we are discussing are easier said than done. Setting aside bitterness in favor of forgiveness may never feel fully natural, so I'm going to give you an assignment. When will you see your father again?"

"Well, there's nothing planned, but he usually shows up at my sister's house at Christmas, and that's just a couple of weeks away. He'll probably spend a few hours with us."

"Okay. Let's assume you can't feel forgiving for the rest of your life, so take that concern off the table. I want you to begin by focusing on the first hour you two will spend together during your Christmas visit." Larry nodded as Dr. Minirth continued. "Let's suppose he comes over at ten o'clock in the morning. Rather than thinking you've got to accept his hardheadedness for the rest of your life, focus on the hour between ten and eleven."

"That I can do, and I see where you're going. But what should I do after eleven o'clock?"

"Well, you've got a whole new hour in front of you at that point. You get to decide then what you'll do with it. Do you want to argue with him for that hour? Do you want to be patient? Do you have permission to leave his side and be with the kids? Speak pleasantly? It will be up to you. But keep your perspective focused on just that one hour."

Can you do the same? While the task of setting bitterness aside forever in favor of forgiving may seem overwhelming, would you be willing to focus on small windows of time?

What assignment could you give yourself that would remind you that emotional management is accomplished one scene at a time? (For instance, "The next time I'm with my sister I'm going to talk about things other than my past family problems," or "When I'm on the phone with my boss, I'm going to stick to the facts at hand and maintain my sense of resolve for fifteen minutes.")

_____

_____

_____

As you are realizing by now, forgiveness will require a major effort on your part, whether or not others choose to be cooperative. This realization will keep you from being ensnared by their aggravating habits. In the next chapter we will explore how you can further increase your ability to forgive by learning to establish and maintain appropriate boundaries and assertiveness.

4

Assertiveness Helps Forgiveness

Step 4. Learn from your problems by establishing better boundaries.

Coleen Barlow, the mother whose husband had left her for another woman, was talking with her best friend, Katy, one Friday evening over dessert. "Do you remember back in grade school when pranksters would put a 'Kick Me' sign on someone's back?" They both laughed because each of them was the impish type who would still play tricks on one another. Yes, Katy could easily relate. Coleen continued. "Sometimes I wonder if that sign is attached to me whenever I deal with Mark. The guy amazes me in the ways he can dream up aggravations!"

"Don't tell me he's been showing up at your front door with a woman wearing a miniskirt and a Dolly Parton wig and enough makeup to stock the local drugstore. It hasn't gotten that bad, has it?"

She chuckled and said, "It's not quite like that, though I'd better brace myself. He's capable of it! But actually, I'm talking about the general way he treats me. He seems to act like a privileged character whenever he's around me. When he comes to pick up the girls he'll just walk into my house and sit at the kitchen table as if that's his prerogative. Then he might check out the fridge and help himself to whatever he finds. It sounds like a small problem, but I really feel offended. He doesn't seem to realize that he's forfeited the right to do those things. I don't want him milling around in my house!"

"Well, that doesn't surprise me at all," Katy quipped. "After all, Mark never seemed concerned about following any protocol before the divorce. Why should he do it now?"

"But it's been five years! You'd think by now he'd figure out that we have separate lives." Coleen was on a roll now and she had lots to unload. "And another thing. A couple of Saturday afternoons ago he called to tell me he was bringing the kids home a day early. He didn't ask if that would be okay or if I'd even be at home. He just declared what he was going to do and then did it. I think he got into an argument with Rachel and just didn't want to be a dad that day."

"Well, did you talk with him about it later?"

"Of course not. Trying to pin him down for a talk is impossible. I had major plans that night but I had to cancel them so I could stay home with Rachel and Allison. Turns out they were fine and would have managed at home without me, but at the time I didn't know what to expect."

"You know what your problem is, don't you, Hon?"

"Well, I'm sure the good Dr. Katy is about to inform me." They both laughed.

"You're a soft touch. You let people run all over you, then you complain about the tire marks they leave on your chest. You need to toughen up, girlfriend."

A few days later Coleen was in Dr. Carter's office reflecting on her conversation with Katy. "I really think she was right. I *am* too easy, and I don't like what it does to me."

"I'm going to assume that after Mark takes advantage of your niceness, feelings of frustration and resentment creep in. Your mood must turn sour after these episodes."

"You assume correctly. But you know, this is nothing new. All my life I've had experiences in which I felt like others had no hesitation to take advantage of my good nature. Mark did it during our entire fourteen years of marriage, so why should he stop now? Before him, my older brother, Todd, was unmerciful to me. He was constantly harassing me, and my parents seemed helpless to know what to do about it. He bullied them almost as much as he bullied me."

"Let me guess," reflected the doctor. "You learned through your experiences to take the course of least resistance. Fighting back did no good, so you'd try to go with the flow and hope that the circumstance would quickly blow over without too much turmoil."

"That's always been my method," admitted Coleen. "But I can't say that I'm any better off because of it. I've always been taught that I shouldn't respond to evil with evil and that a soft answer turns away wrath. So I'm constantly trying to appease." Then she added, "I think my eagerness to please has made me an angrier woman. I'm getting real tired of being on the receiving end of insensitivity."

Dr. Carter realized there was a direct link between her people-pleasing tendency and her struggle to forgive. "It's hard to forgive when the wrongdoer keeps coming back with more of the problematic behavior. I want us to focus on the idea that your ability to forgive Mark will increase only as you learn to establish and maintain consistent personal boundaries."

When people struggle to maintain a spirit of forgiveness it is commonly caused by an ongoing lack of boundaries. Perhaps your circumstances differ from Coleen's, but you can probably relate to her long-standing frustration of being required to be the good guy while others blindly continue being rude or uncaring or selfish or abusive. Like Coleen you may think, *The more I forgive the more it seems that others treat me badly, as if they know they can get away with it.*

Has this ever happened to you? As you think back upon the wrongs you endured you can probably identify how the wrongdoer did not respect your needs, your feelings, or your perceptions. Your boundaries meant nothing. In your effort to be correct you may have thought, *I'm supposed to forgive.* But in the process you did little to establish some guidelines that would ensure that the wrongdoing would abate.

To get an idea if you tend to have weak boundaries, check each of the following statements that would commonly apply to you:

__ Sometimes I can actually be too cooperative when I don't really communicate my feelings of displeasure or disagreement.
__ Strong-willed people seem to be able to wear down my resistance.
__ I may state my opinions and preferences but that doesn't mean others will listen to me.
__ I don't like conflict, and I'll usually do whatever is necessary to keep it minimal.
__ I have relationships where I put in more effort to make it work than the other person.
__ People would be surprised to learn that I'm not really as upbeat as I appear in public.
__ Too many times I'll say yes when I'd really like to say no.
__ Even in some of my closest relationships I'll sometimes refrain from saying what I really feel.
__ Sometimes it seems that others don't take me very seriously.
__ I feel that people tend to take advantage of my good nature.
__ Too often I feel manipulated by other people.
__ I feel frustrated that people don't consider my needs as well as they should.

We all have had moments when it seemed that others were not attuned to our feelings or needs. So it is normal if you checked some of the above items. But if you checked seven or more, there is a good likelihood that you feel disillusioned in some of your important relationships. It probably indicates that others do not respect your legitimate feelings and needs, meaning they disregard your boundaries. While you cannot change the attitudes and feelings others have toward you, your task can be to monitor your own behavior to determine if you are unwittingly enabling others to persist in their insensitivity.

In what circumstances have you been frustrated with the lack of consideration given to you by others? (For instance, "My in-laws refuse to hear my perspective regarding differences between me and my spouse," or "My mother calls our house constantly, even though we've explained that we can't always give her the attention she requires.")

_____

_____

_____

How have you added to your problem by responding with the "nice-guy" approach? (For instance, "I just can't tell my mother not to call me so often; I try to remain friendly.")

_____

_____

_____

How has this approach harmed your ability to forgive? (For instance, "I keep finding new reasons to be bitter," or "It causes me to wonder if I'll always just have to live with rudeness.")

_____

_____

_____

One of the most commonly quoted Scripture passages about forgiveness is Ephesians 4:32: "And be kind to one another, tenderhearted, forgiving one another, even as God in Christ forgave you."

People like Coleen will focus on this verse and say, "See, the Bible says I'm supposed to be kind and tenderhearted so I can forgive. It wouldn't be right for me to become a mean-spirited shrew."

It's true, kindness and tenderness are highly desirable traits that can ultimately be integral to the life committed to forgiveness. But let's put this instruction in its fuller perspective. The verse just prior to this one (Eph. 4:31) instructs us to put away bitterness, wrath, anger, clamor, evil speaking, and malice. Then prior to this verse is another, Ephesians 4:26, which instructs us to be angry without sin. Then yet another prior verse (Eph. 4:15) refers to speaking truth in love.

When you put these other verses into a perspective with the teaching to be kind, tenderhearted, and forgiving, you will realize that forgiveness is possible *as long as* you are correctly managing your anger and taking measures to minimize mistreatment.

Healthy Anger and Boundaries

In a perfect world, you would have no use for anger. If cooperation, courtesy, and respect were the norm, you would find kindness and tenderness to be a natural by-product. Of course, this being a very imperfect world, you feel violated, you hurt, you are at times perplexed and confused. Anger, then, becomes a necessary response for the purpose of preserving legitimate needs and convictions.

As we consider here the necessity of using healthy anger, first pause to reflect about your understanding of this emotion. What image typically comes to mind as you think of anger? (For instance, "I think of shouting and disrespectful behavior.")

_____

_____

_____

In your past, what inhibited you from expressing the full extent of your anger? (For instance, "My dad was rageful, so I determined never to be like him," or "I was specifically told that I'd better keep my anger to myself; no one wanted to hear it.")

_____

_____

_____

Most people we counsel have had great difficulty in understanding healthy anger. Because this emotion can be so unruly and produce so much pain, it is easy to assume that it should be avoided at all costs. Indeed, the Bible does instruct that we should stay away from the loud and quarreling forms of anger. (Look once again at Ephesians 4:31.) But let's make sure we don't swing the pendulum so far away from unruly anger that we lose sight of the good that can come from anger without sin.

Dr. Carter explained to Coleen, "As you describe your ongoing relationship with Mark, I'm hearing that your anger covers a broad spectrum. Sometimes it's mild in the form of minor frustrations or annoyances, and sometimes it reaches a major peak as it turns into an inner rage or hate."

She nodded as she admitted, "I've had so many mood swings with him that the intensity of my emotions runs the full gamut. Sometimes I scare myself because of the frequency of my anger."

"And in the meantime," added Dr. Carter, "when you try to forgive you find that you can't because you keep bumping into those experiences of unresolved anger." She nodded agreement.

"Let me put your thoughts onto an idea that might seem a little odd to you at first," he continued. "I wonder if you would entertain the notion that there is something right and good at the core of your anger. Could you acknowledge that possibility?"

Coleen's eyes widened as her head drew back. "Well, I'm not sure," she said hesitantly. "I guess there's something right about my anger, although I'm not exactly sure what it would be."

"Take a look at the examples you've shared with me," he prodded. "There have been numerous times when Mark has ignored your requests to refrain from having free reign in your house, and there have been times when he irresponsibly tried to make you take over the parenting chores he didn't want to be bothered with. In those incidences, what's right about your feeling of anger?"

"Well, I guess it's normal that I'd want him to be more respectful of me or to be more personally responsible. Is that what you're getting at?" It was clear that Coleen was not accustomed to thinking this way about her anger.

"That's exactly what I'm getting at. I don't think we can fault you for wanting him to be respectful or responsible. You have reasonable needs and convictions."

Stop here for a moment and reflect upon your anger. Can you think of moments in your life when anger can be legitimate? (For instance, "It's legitimate that I feel angry because my former friend spoke condescendingly about me to some mutual acquaintances," or "It would be wrong *not* to be angered at the abuse I received earlier in my life.")

_____

_____

_____

What *right* message is your anger trying to convey? (For instance, "In my anger I'm seeking some deserved respect," or "Anger is my way of indicating that I stand for virtue.")

_____

_____

_____

Coleen smiled as she discussed with Dr. Carter the legitimacy of her anger. "I've lectured myself for so long not to join the ranks of angry people that I had talked myself into believing that nothing good could come of anger. I guess I've overdone a good thing."

Keeping their discussion in a balanced perspective, Dr. Carter explained, "Sometimes people ask me if they have a right to be angry. My response is to suggest that they set aside their concern with rights and think instead of their responsibility. 'Is it a *responsibility* to be angry?' That's how I try to reframe the question. Sometimes it is not responsible to let anger out because it leads to the exchanging of evil for evil, as you mentioned earlier. But sometimes angry communication is a direct act of responsibility. In some circumstances, your emotions or relationship problems can be resolved only as you speak up about the wrongs in your life."

Consider the wrong that has been committed toward you, then consider how your anger can have a right and legitimate function.

What good might come if you were to be firm in communicating your anger? (For instance, "My ex-husband may be less inclined to take advantage of my good nature," or "I'd establish myself as someone who deserves respect.")

_____

_____

_____

Ways to Establish Right Boundaries

By now it should be clear that proper anger includes the preservation of personal worth, needs, and convictions. To come to terms with wrongdoing, you will need to acknowledge to yourself the legitimacy of this emotion. Without healthy anger you will be imbalanced in your relationships.

As you consider how to communicate anger correctly, you will realize that this communication leads to the establishment of relationship boundaries. By that we mean that you are establishing yourself as separate and distinct from people who could harm you or be insensitive to your needs. You are declaring yourself as a valuable person who should be taken seriously. Unlike the case of aggressive or resentful anger, though, you can choose to communicate your boundaries without condescension or harshness. Your intent need not be mean-spirited, but it can be firm or even unbending when necessary.

There are numerous ways you can manage your anger properly by setting legitimate boundaries. Let's examine five common examples of how you might do that.

1. Learn to Say "No"

How many times have you felt that others imposed their preferences or demands on you? In those instances, how often do you go along with the inconvenience, even though you feel it is a true imposition? Too often? This does not have to be.

Recall Coleen's complaint about the time Mark brought the girls home a day early causing her to cancel previously scheduled plans. If it had been an emergency, she would have been right to adjust; but this was an incident in which Mark simply did not want to be a parent, and he knew Coleen would bail him out, as she had done so many times before. Could Coleen say "No"?

"He always gets grumpy when I refuse his requests," she explained. "It's easier for all of us if I just go along with him."

"Let's rephrase that," said Dr. Carter, "and say it's easier *in the short term* to go along with him; but I'm guessing that in the long run he'll keep imposing on you, leaving you feeling used and making forgiveness even more difficult." Coleen acknowledged this to be exactly the case.

What about you? Are you prone to doing the same? What are some circumstances when you need to say no but don't? (For instance, "I never turn my parents down when they call to say they're coming to stay for a weekend, even though they do this a lot.")

_____

_____

_____

How does this negatively affect your long-term emotional status? (For instance, "I've reached the point where I dread their visits.")

———————————————————————————————————————

———————————————————————————————————————

———————————————————————————————————————

Saying no at the appropriate time is not an offense to be avoided. Sometimes you have legitimate needs or plans that others may not have considered, or perhaps they just don't care about them as you do. While a cooperative spirit is desirable, it need not be accomplished at the expense of inner peace.

When you say no, be prepared for a potentially negative reaction from the other person. We have heard about numerous incidences in which the word *no* prompted others to speak insults, give guilt trips, level accusations. In fact, it is fairly predictable that your boundary may prompt a less-than-wonderful response.

Have you ever had this experience? Think of a situation when *no* drew an unfavorable response. (For instance, "When I told my brother I wouldn't lend him money he went months without talking to me.")

———————————————————————————————————————

———————————————————————————————————————

———————————————————————————————————————

Does this negative response cause you to lose your resolve? If you are right and responsible in saying no, then stand firm. You won't necessarily need to explain or defend your actions since this will probably be met with predictable rebuttals. Let your *no* mean *no,* plain and simple.

What attitude adjustment would you need to make as you brace for the negative repercussions from saying no? (For instance, "I'd have to warn myself in advance that I'm not trying to win a popularity contest," or "I'd have to learn to live with gaps in our relationship.")

---

2. Do What You Know Is Right, Even if Others Don't Agree

A woman once spoke with Dr. Minirth about a controversy she was embroiled in with her brother. In the past when the brother's family had stayed in her home, he treated her so rudely that it took days for her to recover from the emotional fallout. Now the brother was wanting to stay in her home while they were in town to attend a wedding. This woman had had such distasteful experiences with the brother that she decided to reserve a room for him at a nearby motel. The brother responded with great anger and chided her for not fulfilling her family obligations. Was she wrong, she asked the doctor, to tell the brother that he could not stay in her home because of the extent of his rudeness in the past?

"You've tried to explain to your brother many times how his behavior affects you," Dr. Minirth summarized as she nodded agreement. "Yet he persists with his insensitive treatment."

"He'll never change because he won't listen, and he believes he's never wrong."

"Then he has forfeited the right to expect favored treatment. While I agree that it would be best if he could stay in your home, I also agree that you have a need to protect yourself from ongoing disrespect. Sometimes you have to make an unpopular decision and stick to it."

If you have had a serious enough problem with someone that forgiveness is necessary, it is predictable that your resolve may be tested. At times you may need to show through your actions that you are firmly committed to fair play, to the extent that you will not be forced to abide by decisions that are ultimately going to be harmful to you. If this requires that you choose a path for yourself that does not coincide with another's wishes, so be it.

In what circumstances are you expected to go along with choices inconsistent with your needs or beliefs? (For instance, "My husband expects me to go to company functions that always turn into drunken parties," or "I've been asked to tell a 'white lie' to cover a family embarrassment.")

_____

_____

_____

How does this pressure impact your effort to be forgiving? (For instance, "It causes resentment to grow," or "It creates a feeling of disrespect in me toward the other person.")

_____

_____

_____

What separate action do you need to implement as you seek to maintain emotional balance? (For instance, "I need to give myself permission to stay home rather than joining in the behavior I disagree with.")

_____

_____

_____

Ultimately you will need to maintain a first priority to healthy living that will include honesty, integrity, and fair-mindedness. Unfortunately, you cannot always count on others to hold the same priorities or to have the same understanding of circumstances. Your task, then, will be to remain true to solid convictions in the hope that your actions may ultimately communicate the truth in ways that words may not accomplish.

3. Know When to Admit Your Limits, Asking for Help When Necessary

As Coleen spoke with Dr. Carter about the idea of setting boundaries she admitted, "I've needed to do what you are suggesting for a long time, but I put it off because it is so unnatural to me. All my life I've been so inclined to meet the needs of others that it feels strange to stake out my own needs."

"No doubt, it's good that you would want to be tuned in to the needs of others," Dr. Carter acknowledged. "After all, service is a trait that some people just don't believe in. But as is so often the case, it's possible to have too much of a good thing. Has it ever occurred to you that you may be guilty of overextending yourself?"

"In my idealistic younger years, I would have thought not," Coleen said. "I always felt it was my duty to push myself to keep people pleased. But now I'm seeing that I've gotten to a place of emotional burnout. I can't keep pushing myself if I expect to find emotional balance."

"A common problem exists with people who have poor boundaries," the doctor explained. "In trying to be too nice you overlook the fact that you're limited in what you can do. Though you may know in your mind that you can't do it all, that inner voice keeps pushing you to go farther. I'm wanting you to realize that it's okay and even necessary for you to declare your limits. Not only is it *not* irresponsible to say 'I'm in need,' it's also more honest."

As we counsel people like Coleen who have difficulty in forgiving we often find that they are setting themselves up for ongoing tension because they won't say, "I'm hurting" or "I need help." We teach them that such an open admission can be crucial to the forgiveness process because it removes the frustrations that can result from feeling as though no one knows or cares about their needs.

How about you? Do you find it hard to admit your limits? To ask for help? In what circumstances do you overextend yourself, even to the point of suppressing legitimate needs? (For instance, "When my friends ask how I'm doing I'll say I'm fine even though I'm really hurting," or "I don't want to sound ungrateful when I visit my mother so I'll try hard to do what she wants, never asking for any personal favors.")

_____

_____

_____

How does this hinder your ability to forgive? (For instance, "No one knows how much pain I carry because of their lack of help or support.")

_____

_____

_____

What personal limits would you like others to recognize in you? (For instance, "I can't always baby-sit the grandkids when asked," or "Sometimes I'm so emotionally wrung out that I need some help just getting routine chores accomplished.")

_____

_____

_____

It is sad but true that most people will not take the time to contemplate your feelings and how they can help you. That being the case, the responsibility rests on your shoulders to educate others regarding your needs. This may require firm unapologetic speech, and it may require that you choose not to backpedal once you've expressed yourself. Are you up to it?

4. Confront Problems as They Arise

A necessary ingredient in establishing boundaries is immediacy. Usually the inability to forgive is heightened by the passing of time. The longer you go before standing up for your convictions, the more difficult it will be to accurately address the problem. Time has a way of muddling memories and watering down the sense of resolve you may need in standing up for yourself.

Coleen, for instance, had a knack for thinking about what she wanted to tell Mark a day or two after he had acted insensitively. Of course, by the time she tried to express her concerns, it was usually too late to be effective.

Dr. Carter mentioned, "I know you can't read the future and predict when Mark may irritate you next, but you could probably do a better job of being on your toes when there is a possibility that you might be manipulated. When are you most likely to have run-ins with him?"

"Almost always when he picks up the girls for an outing he'll do something to throw a kink into our plans. Like recently, the girls were excited because he was going to pick them up to take them to the state fair, but thirty minutes prior to going he called and said it would be another three hours before he could get there. It threw our Saturday morning off completely, and once again we had to accommodate him. This has happened so many times it's ridiculous."

"Did you say anything to him about it?"

"No, I couldn't because I didn't want Rachel and Allison to see us arguing."

"I can appreciate your concern about not wanting to play out your tension in front of your daughters. They don't need any more strain between you two than is already there. Yet, for the sake of conviction, you may need to excuse the girls for a moment so you can talk privately with Mark. You'll not need to make a scene, but you can still address your issues while they are current."

When are you most likely to let problems pass, even if it means letting ill feelings fester? (For instance, "My adult son is irresponsible with money, and I'm constantly bailing him out, but we rarely talk about my feelings," or "At work, I'm the one who's called on to solve someone else's problem, then I get behind in my own projects.")

_____

_____

_____

Why do you procrastinate talking about your needs? (For instance, "I just can't stand dissension," or "The other person won't listen anyway.")

_____

_____

_____

How could your emotions become cleansed if you were more immediate in addressing your needs? (For instance, "I wouldn't waste days brooding over my problems," or "I'd be taken more seriously by others.")

_____

_____

_____

5. Establish Consequences When Necessary

At this point you may be thinking, _This is all well and good. I know I should be more open about my needs, but the person I'm up against is not the understanding type. I don't know if I'll ever succeed in getting my point across._

As you establish assertive boundaries, cling to the idea that talk is cheap. Action is necessary. It may not be easy or pleasant for you to back up your words with actions, but with some people, no other avenue will work. For instance, Coleen decided that she would keep her front door locked when Mark came to her house to pick up the girls. Rather than having him milling around in her kitchen she told him he'd have to wait outside if he was early and they were not ready.

On another matter Mark would let the girls' medical bills go unpaid, knowing Coleen would eventually pick up the tab. In an uncharacteristic move, she gave the medical office his insurance information and his address and let them deal with him directly. Once he was turned in to a collection agency and it made him angry, but he got the point and paid the bills.

Have you ever been in circumstances where words were not enough? When have you had to establish firm consequences in order to get your point across? (For instance, "I finally had to cancel the Visa card that my college daughter was abusing," or "I chose not to go to the Christmas dinner because my dad refused to give up his alcoholism.")

_____

_____

_____

Establishing consequences is usually very unpleasant, particularly if you're already the type of person who has been a peace-at-any-cost player. Yet in some instances it may be the only way to be taken seriously. Unfortunately, some people can be extremely manipulative or insensitive, meaning your well-chosen words will go right past them. Your firmness might not be warmly greeted, yet it may be necessary so you can move forward in your forgiveness.

This brings us to one last point about assertive boundaries.

It's Not Your Job to Make Others Like Your Boundaries

Wouldn't it be nice if your assertive efforts were universally met with appreciation and understanding? Wouldn't you feel relieved if you could express your needs knowing that the one receiving your words would respond with maturity and insight? What a fantasy!

In some cases we have worked with people who have set firm boundaries as part of their effort to forgive, and their efforts were met with acceptance and repentance. Those are the easy cases.

In many instances, however, we have agonized with persons who have felt like lone warriors because they knew their efforts to be healthy would be met with ridicule or rejection. Because wrongdoers would need to exercise humility in order to receive your communications, and because pride and ego are inevitably linked with their wrong deeds, it is unnatural for many of them to maintain the necessary attitude as you establish your boundaries. This means you may have to follow through on your plans knowing it could create discomfort.

Are you up to it? What discomforts might you encounter as you choose to be appropriately assertive? (For instance, "My sister can be very abrasive and will hold back nothing in her reprimands of me," or "I don't want my ex-husband to hate me any more than he already does; he'll be very rigid when we're around each other.")

_____

_____

_____

In order to hold firmly to your convictions you may need to let go of any fantasies regarding a wonderful reception from the wrongdoer. You may be required to acknowledge the ugly truth that others can remain stubbornly committed to inappropriate behaviors and attitudes. Foremost among the fantasies you will have to release is the assumption that you can actually rearrange the thinking of the other person. *You can't.*

You may be required to delicately detach from the person you are setting boundaries with. By this we mean that you would disconnect your sense of contentment from that person's response. For example, Coleen had refused in the past to set boundaries with Mark because she had desperately hoped her cooperative spirit would convince him that she was really a good person. Instead, he took it to mean she was a patsy who could be walked on. No matter how hard she tried she could not make him think as she wanted.

Coleen was finally able to come to terms with her forgiveness toward Mark only as she let go of the hope that she could make him appreciate her needs. Instead of being committed to being extra nice, she became committed to being healthy, even if it meant he would not agree or understand.

Perhaps you will face the same task and similar difficult choices. You may not win any popularity contest, at least not in the mind of the wrongdoer, but that is not your goal. Choose to be committed to clean and fair behaviors and communications, knowing that this may be the necessary ingredient for you to be permanently forgiving and healthy.

5

Assuming Equality

Step 5. Refuse to be in the inferior position and resist the desire to be superior.

Marcia sat in the motel room with her cousin, Sheree, who was also her lifelong best friend and confidante. They had met in Marcia's hometown for a family reunion, and while she had warned herself not to get upset by her father she, nonetheless, had succumbed to his condescending treatment.

"I've been humiliated by that man for the very last time!" Her face was red and her jaw clenched. "He may do a good job of presenting himself to the community as an upright citizen but that man has no comprehension of decency or fair play. I've had it up to here with him! I'm no longer the little girl who'll bow to his bullying and threats. I'm a grown woman who expects to be treated like an adult!"

A few weeks earlier, Marcia's mother, a saint to anyone who knew her, had called to ask her to attend the reunion. Marcia's first instinct was to say no because she couldn't tolerate being with her father for a three-day weekend. But Mother could be persuasive, and besides, she's such a sweet person that her pleas prevailed.

Marcia had arrived at her parents' home at lunchtime on Friday and within minutes the mood for the weekend was set. Instead of a warm hello, her father greeted her with, "What are you doing here so early? Everybody else is coming in tomorrow." That shouldn't have surprised Marcia since Dad was never known for his tact, but it hurt nonetheless.

Her mother, pleasantly plump with round rosy cheeks, had plenty of work to do preparing ham, turkey, vegetable casseroles, and pies, so Marcia busied herself helping in the kitchen. Though she had worked in accounting jobs during the thirteen years since graduating college, Marcia had never lost her domestic side. She loved to cook, and spending time in the kitchen with Mom was a good way to relax and get caught up on news and gossip.

Her first run-in with Dad came Friday evening at suppertime. Being tired because of her busy day, Mom had said to her husband, "Olin, let's run out real quick for a bite to eat at the Country Grill. I've been slaving all day at the stove, and I'd like to let someone else serve me supper."

"I knew you'd ask to go out," he grumbled. "You know how I like to spend Friday nights at home. I don't know why you think that just because you've had a busy day you've got to slack off and go out for dinner. Why can't you just throw something together real quicklike?"

A look of disgust crossed Marcia's face. "Dad, why can't you be a little more understanding? It's no big deal that we want to go out for supper. Besides, if it's your pocketbook you're worried about, I'll pay."

"Now you listen to me, young lady. I'll not have you coming into my house telling me how the cow eats the cabbage. You may be some high-and-mighty professional woman, but when you're back at my house you'd better remember who calls the shots."

Marcia persuaded her mother to go out for supper but Dad stayed home. Through the course of the evening, Marcia fumed with anger while Mom fidgeted under the weight of guilt for leaving her husband behind.

The next day their problems continued. Dad pointed out to Marcia that she'd been putting on too much weight. He tried to give her advice about her money management. He told her that at her age it was a crime to be single. Then he largely ignored her (or perhaps it would be more accurately stated that he snubbed her) as the family members began arriving for the Saturday afternoon and evening festivities. The mood between father and daughter was so frigid by Saturday night that Marcia pounced on her cousin Sheree's invitation to stay with her at the local motel.

"Why don't you confront your dad about the way he treats you?" Sheree asked as they sat on the motel beds in their nightwear. "He's treated you like this for as long as I can remember. Something's got to give!" Sheree truly loved her cousin, and she hated seeing her hurt.

"Believe me, I've tried, but nothing gets through his thick skull. I don't guess I've ever told you because I've been ashamed to talk about it, but ten years ago I had a major confrontation with him. I told him then that I had very painful memories of his verbal abuse and his constant put-downs. When I was twelve there were three or four incidents where he tried to fondle me, so I brought that up in our discussion as well. It really made him furious for me to say what I did, and he went months without talking to me, but I didn't really care. I'd said what I needed to say."

"Well, he certainly doesn't seem to have changed much," Sheree observed. "Maybe it's time for another talk. There's no reason for him to carry on like this."

"I've toyed with the idea," Marcia admitted, "but I don't know if it would do any good. For a couple of years Dad backed off of his high-and-mighty ways, but as time has continued he's just gone back to more of his old tactics. I think he's got a permanent case of pig-headedness."

Marcia's father struggled with a problem common to most troublemakers. He had an insatiable need to be in the superior position.

81

That is what was behind his critical remarks and his power communication to his wife and daughter. Though he would never admit it to anyone, his efforts to be superior were a cover for his deep struggles with inferiority. He was a man who kept his ego buoyed by looking down upon them, never able to admit his own faults but readily finding fault in others.

Have you ever known such a person? If you are seeking to be forgiving you have probably experienced something similar to Marcia's plight. While, of course, your circumstance will vary, you can undoubtedly recall times when you felt someone else was looking upon you as inferior.

Describe your problem circumstances with someone looking upon you as inferior. (For instance, "My former business partner can't see anything right in the way I handle my business," or "My ex-wife is haughty toward me whenever we're in contact with each other.")

_____

_____

_____

Like Marcia, you have probably grown weary of this treatment. How does this affect you as you try to maintain a forgiving spirit? (For instance, "I start out with good intentions, but I become very discouraged that our problems can't be resolved," or "In my mind I nurture very critical thoughts.")

_____

_____

_____

Being Able to Spot the Superiority Game

As you determine to be a forgiving person you will need to identify how others try to maintain a superior attitude over you and you will need to choose the best path of response. Only in rare circumstances can you expect to communicate your awareness of this problem in hopes of leading to a remedy. More likely, you will need to determine within yourself how you plan to respond to such treatment, even if the wrongdoer never changes.

In order to determine if you have been treated as an inferior person, check the following items that apply to you. As you respond to these items, keep in mind the circumstances that call for you to be forgiving.

___ When I have attempted to discuss my problems or concerns, I have received a steady diet of rebuttals.

___ Others try to motivate me with unnecessary guilt trips.

___ I am weary of the many incidences when others won't accept my feelings as legitimate.

___ Too often I feel as if I'm the only one willing to be flexible or cooperative.

___ There are people in my life who don't like it when I choose my own way.

___ I contend with key people who seem incapable of change.

___ The persons who have wronged me seem to cling to a haughty spirit.

___ I am amazed at how insensitive others can be.

___ I've struggled with people who disregard truth or twist facts to suit their cause.

___ People who have let me down have, nonetheless, portrayed themselves as upright and fair.

___ The persons who have harmed me are known for being critical.

___ The wrongdoers in my life seem to hunger for power and control.

How did you do? If you checked six items or more you are likely to be ensnared in games of one-upmanship. While you may have sincere intentions to forgive, your plans may regularly be sidetracked

83

as you are reminded of your lowly status in the eyes of the wrong-doer.

Marcia's strain with her father was so severe that she sought counseling with Dr. Carter. She gave him details of a family history in which abuse and invalidation were common. Clearly, her father had emotional problems, but as a girl Marcia was not sophisticated enough to understand how to disentangle from his inappropriate messages. Because she saw him as "The Authority," she had accepted his rejection and negative pronouncements as true.

"One of the adjustments we're going to pursue is to reorient you to the truth," Dr. Carter explained. "When you were a girl you learned to think of your father as superior and yourself as inferior. I want you to understand that such teaching was entirely wrong. You have equal worth to anyone. As you go about forgiving you'll need to sidestep your father's messages regarding your inferiority, and you'll also need to refrain from the temptation to hold yourself above him."

"I do a pretty good job of feeling okay about myself," Marcia said, "until I get back into situations where my dad pushes my buttons. It's like he knows just what to say and how to say it, and soon I'm hurt and angry and confused. I lose my resolve to be steady and get pulled right down into his schemes."

Marcia's plight was certainly not rare. In God's perfect design, key people are designated to communicate to you the message of your worth, your competence, and your desirability. Those people include mother, father, spouse, close friends, and church leaders. When God's truth is consistently spoken and portrayed, your ability to manage conflicts and the resulting emotions will be strong. But when you have not had adequate experience in learning God's truth, the result can be emotional confusion.

In what key relationships have you not had sufficient experience in learning about your worth and adequacy? (For instance, "My

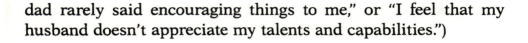

dad rarely said encouraging things to me," or "I feel that my husband doesn't appreciate my talents and capabilities.")

How have these experiences hindered you in your efforts to be forgiving? (For instance, "Before I forgive I want my father to apologize, and he won't," or "I guess I'm waiting for my husband to give me credibility, and it isn't going to happen.")

"Let's understand," Dr. Carter explained to Marcia, "that all people struggle with inferiority feelings to some degree. When you were a child you realized very early that others had skills and abilities that you could not match, so you naturally developed questions about your abilities. Through your developmental years, Mom and Dad needed to talk with you about your question marks. They needed to explain to you and show you, through their actions, that you were not at all inferior."

Marcia interrupted. "Well, maybe that's what they were *supposed* to do, but that's a far cry from what happened. We didn't discuss personal matters at all."

"And that's my point. Instead of guiding you away from your feelings of inferiority, you were left on your own to figure out as best as possible how you would manage your emotions. Unfortunately, most kids aren't very sure of the ways to resolve those kinds of problems, and that's when unhelpful emotional patterns become prominent."

When you were a child, what feelings of inferiority did you struggle with? (For instance, "My brother constantly made me feel inadequate," or "I felt that I was supposed to make all A's before I could claim any worth.")

_____

_____

_____

How did your family help you sift through your emotions? (For instance, "I was just told to quit whining and act right," or "My mother tried to get me to think about positive things so I could just get my mind off my problems.")

_____

_____

_____

Most adults looking back on their childhoods recall few times when their emotions were clearly resolved. Certainly this was the case with Marcia. Then bad habits tend to form, and it's these habits that eventually hinder you as an adult as you try to come to terms with the maltreatment you received. During early development there are two general ways in which people respond to feelings of inferiority: (1) They acquiesce to the lower position, or (2) They try to find ways to feel superior.

Accepting an Inferior Status

The first bad habit that befalls many is to accept personal inferiority as a fact. You may have reasoned, "If significant people treat me as if I'm no good, I guess they're right." In Marcia's case, she had grown so accustomed to being put down that she assumed she was, indeed, inadequate.

She explained, "I can distinctly remember thinking that I had no business expecting valued treatment because my dad was so hard on me. When people _did_ treat me well I didn't trust it."

You can tell if you have accepted inferiority as fact if you are prone to any of the following:

- You can be too easily motivated by guilt and duty.

- You feel you've got to explain yourself thoroughly to others.

- You work too hard to justify yourself.

- Your feeling of stability lasts only as long as you are approved by others.

- You apologize too readily for things that don't really require an apology.

- You adjust your behavior based on the possible judgments you might receive.

- You use the word *can't* frequently.

- You somehow let people dominate you or manipulate you.

- You try too hard to be a people-pleaser.

In what ways do you most commonly succumb to feelings of inferiority? (For instance, "I accept blame for problems I didn't create," or "I don't give myself credit for having capable skills.")

_____

_____

_____

Attempting to Be Superior

The second way people respond to their feelings of inferiority is to attempt to hold themselves above others. The reasoning goes something like this: "I'm tired of people treating me lowly. It's my turn to show them that I'm better than they are."

Marcia grinned slyly as Dr. Carter asked, "Have you ever thought to yourself that you just wouldn't take your father's abuse, so you'd find ways to put him in his place, just as he's done to you?"

"You might say I've got a feisty streak. I can only be put down so much until I decide it's time to fight back. I remember particularly as a teenager I decided *not* to just lie down and let my father walk all over me. I had some moments when I really gave it to him."

She went on to describe some of her behavior toward him. She argued back, frequently pointing out his bad logic. She said harsh, hurtful things to him. She deliberately did what he told her not to do, though he frequently did not know about it. She spoke ill of him to her friends. She tuned him out during his scolding lectures. She refused to answer when he tried to get her to talk.

Can you blame Marcia for wanting to separate herself from her father's harsh treatment? Not really. In her spirit she knew he was wrong to belittle her as he did, so it was good that she had enough spirit to say "Enough." Yet, in her angry responses to her father she made the mistake of trading places with him (she was feeling superior and he was being deemed inferior), but in doing so *she was still playing his game.* Their relationship resembled a playground seesaw; one would be in the up position then would go down as the other went up. They had a never-ending competition to determine who would hold himself or herself above the other.

Temporarily, her attempts to be superior over her father would bring a type of relief, but over the course of many years, Marcia was still struggling to find emotional peace. Compensating for inferiority by attempting to be superior may create short-term satisfaction, but it yields long-term strife.

You can know that you are probably compensating for inferiority with false superiority if you find yourself exhibiting any of the following:

- You cling to judgmental thoughts and feelings about the other person.

- Your communication is an effort to outargue or persuade.

- You punish people with silence or withdrawal.

- You hold on to grudges, not letting go of pain or hurt that may have originally been legitimate.

- You try to prove yourself by being an overachiever.

- You won't accept any input about ways in which you may be in error.

- You can tear to shreds another person's reasoning.

- You develop patterns of stubbornness or hardheadedness.

Consider your efforts to compensate for inferiority by becoming superior. What behaviors have you used to accomplish this? (For instance, "I'll quickly invalidate my sister when she speaks in emotionally charged ways toward me," or "I'm constantly thinking how my logic is far better than the logic of my former employer, to the point that I obsess too much about it.")

_____

_____

_____

How does your attempt at superiority hinder your forgiveness process? (For instance, "I'll have to be honest and admit I enjoy looking down on my ex-husband," or "It keeps me caught in my anger.")

_____

_____

_____

Marcia (and perhaps you too) fluctuated back and forth between feeling inferior and striving to be superior, and it was getting her nowhere. Dr. Carter explained to Marcia, "I can understand how your history of abuse has caused you to question your adequacy, and I can appreciate why you would want to compensate by elevating yourself above your father. But there's a third option I'd like to see you try as you come to terms with his mistreatment of you."

Marcia was ready for something different, so she heard him out. "I'd like you to consider that you're neither inferior nor are you superior to anyone. I wonder if you'd be willing to entertain the notion that you are equal to any person who crosses your path. That would allow you to stay clear of anyone's invitation to think lowly of yourself, but this belief would also keep you from lording yourself unnecessarily over anyone, as well."

While all humans are inferior to God's standard of perfection, no human was ever intended by the Creator to be held in higher or lower esteem to another human. God's plan is for equality among individuals. While we each differ with respect to skills and achievements and gifts, we each hold a similar core value in His eyes. The apostle Peter struggled with feelings of superiority over the centurion Cornelius. But finally as God showed how He loved them both Peter concluded, "In truth I perceive that God shows no partiality" (Acts 10:34).

"In theory, this sounds pretty good," said a skeptical Marcia, "but I'm not real sure I'm ready to do everything it implies. Are you saying that after all of the ways my father has manipulated me and put me down I'm supposed to consider him my equal?"

"I'm saying that he was wrong, and continues to be wrong, to hold himself above you. And just as you don't want him to lord over you, it's appropriate to ask you not to do the same to him."

Forgiveness can only occur as you lay down the temptation to repay evil with evil. Is it evil for a human to abuse and mistreat another human? Yes, and such behavior requires a label of wrong. Is it best to respond to the evil with begrudging and condescension?

No, this would only put you on par with the very mistreatment from which you want distance.

Let's move forward with a two-part idea: (1) All people are equally in need of God's mercy, and (2) All people are equally loved by God. (People respond *very* differently to God, meaning no two behave exactly alike, but that does not erase the truth that we all begin on the same level.)

In order to come to terms with your equality to others, and therefore to forgive others, there are four key insights to consider: (1) Understand your worth as coming from God, not humans, (2) Come to terms with messages producing false guilt, (3) Learn to detach from others' psychological games, and (4) Learn to communicate as an equal, even when others won't. Let's examine each of these.

Worth Is from God, Not Humans

If you have felt pain because of someone else's mistreatment, you will recognize that at the core of your pain is a protest: "Won't you *please* show me some respect?" When others give you the respect you want and deserve, your emotions settle down. But what do you do when another person will *not* acknowledge your worth? Are you doomed to remain stuck in your pain? This is what seems to be happening to the one who cannot seem to forgive. He or she finds it hard to move forward as long as the wrongdoer deems him or her inferior.

In her motel room conversation with her cousin, Marcia typified the anguish of one yearning to be respected. "Is it wrong," she cried to Sheree, "for me to wish I had a dad who could treat me like a fellow adult? Like someone who has a brain?"

In one of her conversations with Dr. Carter he asked her, "When you were first born, what sort of reception did you receive at the hospital?"

Startled at the question, she stammered, "Well, I don't know, I'm not sure. I guess when I was born I got the usual treatment. The nurses took care of me. My mother smiled a lot. My dad must've called relatives with the news. Is that what you're getting at?"

"Exactly. I'm assuming you were greeted in the same warm fashion virtually every baby experiences at birth. Any reasonable person at that moment was pleased to be part of bringing a new life into the world. The care you received at that moment illustrated that they believed you had value."

Marcia smiled as she replied, "Well, I would hope that was the case!"

"Now let's look at a different angle about that scene. Exactly what had you done at that point in your life to deserve such worthy treatment?"

Another startled look. "Well, uh, actually nothing. I mean, I hadn't had a chance yet to do anything. I was just a baby!"

"Right again. But the people involved realized you were a baby with worth. It had nothing to do with high achievement or good behavior. By virtue of your very existence, and nothing else, you had worth." Dr. Carter paused as Marcia nodded agreement. "Now let's take this thought a little farther. Where do you suppose that worth came from? Who gave it to you?"

She was catching on to his reasoning now. "It had to come from God. It was His birthday gift to me."

"I like the way you think. Now, one more idea. In the years to follow, it was the job of your parents to recognize that worth, draw it out, and show it to you. How successfully was that accomplished?"

"I'd say with my mother, it was very successful. She's the epitome of grace and has a way of putting a positive spin on things. I felt very valued by her." She paused for a moment then said, "Now Dad was a different story. I just don't think he knew how to love."

Let's apply some logic to Marcia's past. On the day of her birth she had worth, a gift from God. Her mother succeeded in showing her that worth, her father did not. Does her father's lack of acknowledgment of her worth subtract from its existence? No, her worth continued to exist whether he could see it or not. The fact that he devalued her distracted her from *feeling* its presence, but it did not cause the worth to cease existing. Once God deems life precious, the words or actions of humans do not make His declarations any less true. Humans may deter you from seeing it, but they cannot change the truth.

Have you had experiences with key people who could not acknowledge your God-given worth? How have you been affected in this way? (For instance, "My brother holds himself in judgment over me, as if he's the one who determines my value.")

_____

_____

_____

How could your emotions be changed for the better if you decided to recognize that humans cannot undo what God has declared to be true? (For instance, "I wouldn't have to filter my self-esteem through my brother's judgments," or "I could chart my life's course on God's plan for me, not on my former friend's bad feelings about me.")

_____

_____

_____

By accepting your worthiness as a truth that cannot be changed, how could you be more capable of forgiving those who have wronged you? (For instance, "I wouldn't need to respond to another person's insults with my own insults in return," or "I'd be free to choose whether I want to remain angry or not, and I'd choose what is best for my personal stability.")

_____

_____

_____

Sidestep Invitations for False Guilt

When you have been wronged by someone else it is very possible that you will then struggle with feelings of shame and guilt. Even when the facts strongly support your innocence, you can still be susceptible to self-doubt. For instance, recall that Marcia's father had been sexually inappropriate with her a few times when she was twelve. Was she in any way at fault for this? Absolutely not. She was an innocent girl who regrettably had to endure the humiliation thrust upon her by a man who was seriously misguided. She had absolutely no guilt in the matter.

Yet as she recalled the circumstances to Dr. Carter she expressed deep shame for her past. "I can't believe I could even be involved in something like that," she cried through her tears. "It's so dirty."

Have you ever felt similar feelings of guilt for the wrongs someone else perpetrated against you? (For instance, "My husband had an affair, but I feel that I somehow should have prevented it," or "I always felt guilty when my mother became drunk.")

_____

_____

_____

When you cling to guilt that does not belong to you, inferiority feelings grow and forgiveness becomes elusive. As long as you accept blame for someone else's wrong, you will consciously or subconsciously cling to a simmering anger and desire for revenge (superiority).

Be objective regarding the facts. If you have done no wrong, then let go of any guilt. And even if you can pinpoint mistakes you made in association with another's wrongdoing, let God forgive you. Commit to a right life and move forward.

What unnecessary guilt thoughts can you choose to release from your mind? (For instance, "Though my marriage has been difficult, I can release myself from self-condemnation because I know I have given it my best effort.")

_____

_____

_____

Dr. Carter told Marcia, "I, too, regret what your father did to you as a girl and what he continues to do to you as an adult. But I'd like you to free yourself from the false guilt that causes you to be less than your best. I want your emotional slate to be clean so you can hold your head high as you consider the values you want to maintain in your life now and in the future."

Think of the pain you have felt because of someone else's insensitivity. Describe what is false about the guilt you've held. (For instance, "I didn't make my husband have an affair, it was his free choice," or "My mother drank for reasons I didn't know about; it was not because of me.")

_____

_____

_____

Now determine what thoughts you could claim in the place of that guilt. (For instance, "I'm still a decent woman in spite of my husband's problems," or "I've responded to my mother's problems by developing a keener sense of my own adult responsibility.")

_____

_____

_____

Can you see that as you absolve yourself of guilt that never was yours in the first place, you can be free to forgive the wrongdoer?

The more clean you feel inwardly the less you will be tempted to hold on to superior thoughts about someone else. Since superiority is a false compensation for feelings of inferiority, your need to "even the score" will decrease as you realize you are, indeed, free from blame for someone else's problems.

Practice Delicate Detachment

In a perfect world you would be able to attach yourself to others through love, knowing you would be greatly blessed for doing so. Since, however, you have not experienced perfection (nor will you ever on this side of heaven) you will encounter circumstances requiring detachment.

When you remain in the inferiority-superiority struggle with your wrongdoer, you remain attached to that person. When that wrongdoer persists in rejecting you or refuses to be fully repentant, your attachment is likely to result in ongoing emotional turbulence.

"I think you can see very clearly," Dr. Carter continued with Marcia, "that your father does not operate with fully healthy characteristics. As a girl you naturally wanted to look up to him, but as an adult you realize he has not lived up to what he could be."

"That's a pretty sad thing to have to admit about your father," she replied, "yet it's totally true. He's just not a likable person much of the time."

"In order to disentangle from his condescensions and to forgive, it'll be necessary for you to detach emotionally from him. You can't afford to stay on the one-up, one-down seesaw."

"I've known that for some time, but how do I do that? I've still got to see him and be in his presence as long as I have a relationship with my mother."

"Your detachment can lead you to make two separate adjustments," explained the doctor. "First, when you're with him, have zero expectations. Don't go in hoping and expecting him to be any different than he has been. Second, cease any communication that is persuasive toward him. Any pleas or convincing statements keep you engaged in ways that will perpetuate frustration."

"Easier said than done! I guess I've held a fantasy that somehow, someway, I could make him see the light. But you're saying he probably won't change. I know you're right, but I also know that if I do this, a dream within me will have to die, the dream of having a normal dad. That's tough!"

In what ways will you need to do the same as Marcia, practicing delicate detachment? (For instance, "I need to quit thinking I can make my ex-husband act kindly toward me," or "I need to allow my mother-in-law to be the bossy, opinionated person she is, even if it requires me to spend less time with her.")

_____

_____

_____

By suggesting detachment, we are not suggesting that you become harshly rejecting. (That is why we call it *delicate* detaching.) We are suggesting, though, that even when persons persist in holding themselves as superior to you, you do not have to respond in kind.

Communicate as an Equal

As the Christmas holidays approached, Marcia and Dr. Carter talked about her anticipated interactions with her family. "I'm going to spend some time with Sheree, so that will be positive; and Mother and I will do lots of shopping, which we enjoy." Then she sighed heavily. "But of course, I'll still have Dad to contend with and I don't want him to ruin our holidays."

"Well, we can't predict what he might do, so be prepared. One thing is certain. Based on past history he'll probably speak down to you or your mother several times. Your job is to refrain from jumping onto the seesaw with him, playing right into his manipulations."

"I guess this means I'd better not say a word to him, huh? That's about the only way I'll stay clear of trouble."

"Let's say you have permission not to be chatty with him if you know it's only going to produce pain. But I'm also hoping you can speak to him adult-to-adult rather than the parent-to-child manner he's more accustomed to."

The two spelled out her possible responses to potential scenarios.

- If her father insulted her about her appearance, she could firmly state, "I'm comfortable with the way I look, so it's not an issue to me."

- If he tried to dictate her schedule she could reply, "I've already got my day planned." (No further explanation would be required.)

- If he complained about a Christmas gift she would reason, "There's always the option of exchanging it for something you might like better."

Marcia's plan was to sidestep his invitations for argumentative exchanges. If he felt the need to look down on her, that was his prerogative. She had decided that in spite of his wish to be above her, she would consider herself an equal whether he liked it or not.

And you? Write down three or four possible scenarios in which a wrongdoer may try to put you in a place of lower status. (For instance, "My brother may pick apart my manner of parenting," or "My boss may speak ill of me to coworkers.")

_____

_____

_____

_____

Now go back through each of those possible circumstances and write a response that would indicate your view of yourself as an equal, not a subordinate. (For instance, "When my brother criticizes, I can continue my parenting style with no defense, knowing he has the right to be wrong.")

_____

_____

_____

_____

Remember that others' immaturity does not mandate your misery. When possible, it would be good to talk with your wrongdoer about joining you in positive adjustments to your relationship. (We'll discuss this further in Chapter 8.) In the meantime, refuse to try to win psychological games that have no winner, only losers.

6

Refraining from Judgments

Step 6. Avoid the futility of judgments, letting God be the ultimate judge.

"Do you want to know what drives me stark-raving mad?" Daniel had brought in his dump truck of emotional garbage to Dr. Minirth's office. "Here I am finally admitting that I have a problem with alcoholism. I'm being honest with myself about this problem for the first time in my life. But what do I get from my wife and her parents and my parents? I get judgment, that's what!"

"How do they judge you?"

"Well, first my mother piously tells me I should never have touched a drop of alcohol, ever, as if I were some schoolboy who didn't know any better. My dad tells me he's disappointed in me, that he had hoped for more than this from his son. My wife says she can't trust me because I'm a liar. And her parents won't talk to me because of the embarrassment I've put the kids through.

"But you know the part that hurts the most?" Daniel was really peeved. "I know something about every one of them that could put them to shame, and I don't judge *them*. My dad once had a girlfriend on the side that my mother still doesn't know about to this day. My mother pops Valium and painkillers like they were candy. My wife used to be bulimic, and the reason for it was traced back to her parents who look nice to everyone on the outside, but at home they're rigid and controlling. They have no clue about how to love."

Then adding extra emphasis to his complaints, he added, "And every one of them claims to be a Christian, which means they ought to know better. Seems to me there's something in the Bible that says 'judge not.' But I guess they conveniently forget what they don't want to do."

Anger and hurt showed all over Daniel's face. Forty-four years old, his life had been a series of peaks and valleys. When life was good, it could be very good. A dozen years earlier he was making a large income in commercial real estate, lived in an expensive home, drove the nice cars, took his wife, Belinda, on regular getaway vacations to the lake. He was respected at church and had served on the finance committee for years. Friends looked up to him and asked his advice on business matters. He was known as truly reliable.

But when life was bad it got really bad. He lost his business when the economy hit a slowdown and was forced into the humiliation of bankruptcy. He downsized into a smaller home and more modest cars, yet even then he struggled to make financial ends meet. His only son, Brian, became rebellious during his early teens, forcing Daniel and Belinda to put him into counseling and academic tutoring they couldn't afford. Because of his downturn he withdrew from church involvement, knowing people there had lost respect for him. It was then that his modest social drinking turned into daily indulgences and increasingly frequent binges.

When he finally sought help from Dr. Minirth, Daniel had hoped he would receive the support of family and friends. Instead, his admission of personal problems opened a floodgate of pent-up anger from the very people whose love he wanted most. As a result, he was burdened mightily with disillusionment, depression, and despair. Forgiving his family for their role in his problems was proving to be difficult because he could not get past the seeming unfairness of their judgmental attitudes.

His wife, Belinda, told him she wanted their marriage to work, *but* (and this is all Daniel heard) she no longer trusted him because he'd been sneaky and dishonest about his drinking and his failing business. He was going to have to prove himself first before she'd risk giving him any signs of hope or words of lasting encouragement.

"What she says was deception, I say was discretion. I wasn't deliberately lying to her about my personal problems. I just didn't want to drag her any deeper than necessary into the holes I'd dug for myself. I'm certainly being honest now, can't she see that? I feel like I've laid myself wide open for the sake of true repentance and introspection, but instead of support, my closest allies have pulled out their bazookas and aimed them directly at me!"

As you might guess, the rest of Daniel's family had a different spin on his story, yet as Dr. Minirth worked with him he realized that Daniel's feelings were not to be discounted. He felt very hurt and embittered because he was being judged for his wrongs. In order for him to progress he would need to come to terms with those judgments. Would he let judgments rule his emotions, or could he chart his own separate course toward healing and a forgiving spirit? That was Daniel's dilemma.

Perhaps you, too, have known the pain that accompanies judgment. Do you remember the old saying from childhood, "Sticks and stones may break my bones, but words will never harm me?" Well, that's dead wrong! Words of judgment and rebuke *do* harm. They can cut at you like a knife, leaving you with open emotional wounds that take much time and great effort to heal.

Undoubtedly the circumstances that have preceded your need to forgive involved conflict. Anytime conflict arises there are differing perceptions regarding what actually has happened. You may look upon the conflict remembering the way someone mistreated you, yet they may see the circumstances as if *you* were the one in the wrong. Blame, accusation, and judgment can arise from conflicting perceptions, creating a deeper feeling of pain that muddles your ability to forgive.

To determine if judgment is a potential hurdle to your forgiveness process, check each of the following statements that pertain to you.

__ I feel that I just can't please certain key people.
__ It seems that my good accomplishments are overshadowed by the bad.
__ I have felt snubbed by others.
__ No matter how well I explain my feelings or perceptions, I am still met with rebuttals.
__ False things have been said about me behind my back.
__ When others talk about my problems, it seems they overlook their own frailties.
__ Because of a conflict or a mistake, people have deliberately ignored me or withdrawn from me.
__ At times I have an exaggerated desire to explain myself to others.
__ These days I'm not exactly sure who accepts me and who doesn't.
__ I feel as if I am dealing with people whose minds are made up, even though they don't know all the facts.
__ I have experienced incidents when people have talked down to me.
__ I have determined that it's just not safe to be open with many people at all.

How did you do? If you checked six statements or more, it's likely that you are in an environment that feels judgmental. You are more likely to feel defensive, and as a result your ability to move forward toward a forgiving spirit will be deterred.

What has happened in your life that causes people to judge you? (For instance, "My father was a womanizer and I know people wonder about *my* character too," or "In the past I had a nasty temper.")

Knowing you may be judged, how does this negatively affect your
ability to forgive? (For instance, "I'm the kind of person who feels
the need to set the record straight first," or "Plain and simple, I
hate judgmental people.")

Let's underscore a key idea at this point. The presence of a judgmental spirit can, indeed, be annoying and discouraging, but it is not
fatal to your ability to forgive. Forgiveness is a choice you can make
even if the people you are in conflict with do not cooperate. While
you would like a more receptive atmosphere from your significant
others, you can choose forgiveness because of your independent commitment to a right way of life.

In order to separate yourself from others' judgments (and your
own temptation to judge in return) there are two factors that warrant
your attention: (1) The excessive emphasis society places on evaluations, and (2) The universal struggle with sinful pride.

The Evaluation Emphasis

Think back through the years and try to get a handle on the
number of times you've been evaluated. Start with your preschool
days and consider how many times a toddler is told, "Good job"
or "That's wonderful" or "Terrific!" As they first begin assimilating
language, toddlers realize that many behaviors will be evaluated and
judged. They learn to anticipate the pronouncements. At that point
they begin to openly solicit good judgments.

Then progress into your grade school years. What becomes the primary focus as children enter formal education? While the purpose of school is to instruct, many children (perhaps you were one of them) assume that they should get good grades. Making A's is all important. Avoiding F's is paramount. When children talk with their parents about school, the attention readily focuses on bringing the grades up.

During the teen and college years, not only does the emphasis on scholastic grades continue, but many other factors become matters of evaluation. The way you dress is graded, as are your social standing, your extracurricular accomplishments, your hairstyle, and the kind of car you drive, just to mention a few.

Does this tendency toward evaluation cease once you become an adult? Of course not. You continue to be graded for many things: the status of your job, your income level, how well your kids behave, how nice your house looks, how socially adept you are, how good a Christian you are.

Is the picture becoming clear? Grades—evaluations—are so integral to what we are, they can never be avoided. We are programmed throughout life to size up one another.

Through the years, what aspects of your life have been routinely evaluated? (For instance, "I'm constantly graded by my husband on how the house is kept," or "My mother keeps score of the times I lose my temper.")

How have you been influenced by this evaluation? (For instance, "I can be image conscious," or "I try to get people to see my good side while I cover up my bad side.")

What impact does the evaluation emphasis have on your emotions? (For instance, "I'm somewhat guarded, particularly around people who love to hand out grades," or "I feel discouraged because I know I can't live up to others' perfect standards.")

_____

_____

_____

This evaluation emphasis has quite an impact on the forgiveness process. Most people attempting to forgive struggle with one of two problems: (1) They feel upset because they know others give them low grades, or (2) They cannot get past the tendency to evaluate others, meaning they hold the wrongdoer in contempt beyond the point of it being constructive.

Daniel was struggling with the evaluation emphasis in both directions. First, he was angry because his family graded him poorly because of his history of alcoholism and manipulative behavior. Second, in spite of his declaration that he never judged them, he regularly evaluated his family members regarding their weaknesses and their attitudes toward him.

Dr. Minirth talked with Daniel about his reactions to judgments. "I can't blame you for feeling hurt that your family thinks poorly of you right now. My concern for you is heightened because you're letting their judgments rule your emotions, and though you don't want to be judgmental yourself, you're responding in kind. That's only compounding the problem."

Daniel shook his head in frustration. "Ever since I was a kid," he said, "I've been doing whatever it takes to make the grade. I was an honor student in school. I had a reputation as a clean, moral kid. I rarely gave anyone problems. And in my adult life I tried to live by good moral and ethical standards. But when problems surface, boom! Here come the judgments. Suddenly, my good qualities don't count anymore. I'm branded as a loser and I get no respect."

So what's a person like Daniel to do when faced with an onslaught of judgment? What can you do if you are facing similar circumstances? Understand that God, indeed, does not intend for humans to judge humans. He wants us to maintain standards of right and wrong. He wants us to be accountable. He allows us to experience consequences for our poor choices. But He clearly discourages us from sitting in the judgment seat.

In your opinion, why is it best that humans refrain from judging other humans? (For instance, "In spite of differing problems, we're all basically the same," or "No one can perfectly compute why another person makes the mistakes they do.")

_____

_____

_____

What is a better alternative to judgment? (For instance, "I need to be accepted," or "People need to give a helping hand.")

_____

_____

_____

The better alternative to judgment begins with *descriptive thinking*. You can certainly have opinions about right and wrong, but in the end, describe how you feel about circumstances without giving grades.

Dr. Minirth explained it to Daniel this way: "First, I want you to think about the way you'd like your family members to approach you. I'm assuming you can acknowledge that it's realistic that they feel hurt because of their disappointment in you."

"Well, yeah. I mean I'm not asking them to quit feeling what they feel. That's not my beef."

"You'd have an easier time if they could describe to you how they feel and what improvements they'd like to see in their relationships with you. Am I right?"

"Exactly. I *want* to make restitution. I *want* to be trustworthy again. If we could remove the cloud of judgment I think we could make some very real progress."

"Let's put together a plan," suggested Dr. Minirth. "We can't *make* your family stop judging. That's going to be a matter for them to come to terms with on their own. In fact, some of the people you're in conflict with may never cease their judgments. What you *can* do is unhook yourself from the judgments. Realize they're out of line and release yourself from the mandate that you must make an *A* on their report cards. Be honest as you describe to yourself what rights and wrongs have occurred, but don't assume you have to play up to anyone to make the grade."

Chuckling slightly he replied, "Boy, that'd be a relief, although I have a feeling it's easier said than done. This would take a reorienting of my thinking."

What about you? Can you disconnect from others' evaluations and judgments? How could this happen? (For instance, "When I'm around my mother I won't play up to her, trying to get her to think I'm okay," or "When former friends pass rumors about me it won't be necessary to defend every one.")

_____

_____

_____

Of equal importance, you can also choose not to judge the judges. Let descriptive thinking replace your evaluations. What judgments would you be willing to give up? (For instance, "My ex-husband is very condescending to me, but instead of judging I can acknowledge that it makes me feel hurt; then I can let go of the expectation that he will make the grade.")

_____

_____

Letting go of judgments is neither easy nor natural. If you are going to forgive, though, you will need to separate yourself from this mind-set and leave judgments to God.

Daniel confessed, "I've spent my entire life being judged and giving out judgments, and now you're asking me to cease. Man, that's going to feel strange."

"I'm hoping it will also feel good. There is no need to let people pronounce you as good or bad, acceptable or not acceptable. That's for God to do. Likewise, there's no need for you to give it in return. Describe how circumstances make you feel, make choices regarding the direction of those emotions, but sidestep the temptation to play God by giving them the judgments you don't want them to give you."

Then Dr. Minirth added, "That leads to a second key idea I want you to understand. The tendency to judge is part of a deeper problem with pride, which is a major trap to avoid."

Understand the Nature of Pride

When you think of the word *pride*, what comes to mind? Most people assume pride means arrogance or having a haughty spirit, and that is not entirely wrong. Pride can be manifested in those traits, but it is a *much* broader quality than that.

Let's acknowledge first that there is a good form of pride, a feeling of satisfaction and contentment. For instance, you may take pride in your children or in a job well done or in your American citizenship. At such moments, you are experiencing a positive form of pride.

But the pride that accompanies a judgmental spirit is defined as a preoccupation with personal cravings, preferences, and desires. It represents a falsely elevated view of one's self. This pride is at the root of criticism, a rejecting spirit, invalidation, and so forth.

How have others exhibited pride toward you? (For instance, "When my brother refuses to speak to me, he is exhibiting a false, puffed-up sense of self.")

_____

_____
_____
_____

And you? Do you ever respond to someone's pride with your own pride? How might you exhibit this? (For instance, "I get too consumed with my standing with others," or "I respond with my own condescending criticisms.")

_____
_____
_____

Daniel admitted to Dr. Minirth, "You know, I've heard about pride all my life, but I haven't really taken much time to consider how susceptible I am to it. I always assumed that if I didn't draw too much conceited attention to myself, I was avoiding the pride trap."

"I guess you can see now that it's a much bigger issue. In fact, it's everywhere!" the doctor remarked. "It's prideful when people hold themselves in judgment over you, and it's also prideful for you to assume you can judge them regarding the ways they treat you."

Dr. Minirth continued. "I'd like for you to consider how pride's opposite, humility, might cause you to respond very differently when judgmental circumstances are present." When you think of humility, what comes to mind? Weakness? Frailty? Being taken advantage of? If so, you're on the wrong track.

Humility is strength under fire. If pride represents the preoccupation with self, then humility is the lack of self-preoccupation. In humility you are not so concerned with the self's preferences that you cannot make room for situations that run counter to those preferences. And while you may want to maintain a healthy self-esteem, you're not shocked when others choose not to esteem you.

When you embrace humility you can find the strength to disconnect from other folks' judgments. You'll realize:

- You can continue to grow even if a misguided person pridefully gives you an F.

- You gain nothing by being critical or judgmental of others.

- Grades from others are empty. No human has the power of God to know who you really are and how you should be judged.

- You are limited in your ability to make people think well of you.

- Contentment comes from a right relationship with God, not the high opinions of others.

"I'm hoping you can learn some personal lessons as you observe how judgmental people can be toward you," Dr. Minirth explained to Daniel. "It's humbling to realize that your character can be so summarily degraded, but then that's not all bad."

A quizzical look crossed Daniel's face, so the doctor continued. "You mentioned that in the past your self-esteem was anchored in your many accomplishments. In other words, you felt pride, and that became your foundation for personal confidence. Now, though, you don't have that same feeling of accomplishment. Your failures have been exposed for all to see. But in spite of it all, you can still find self-esteem. Only now it won't be anchored in your accomplishments, but in God's declaration of love for you. Contentment can now be spiritually based, not performance based."

Daniel had heard ideas like that for years, but until now they had little relevance to him. "I'm going to really have to think hard about what you're saying." It was clear he was steeped in deep thought. "I know what you're saying is right, but truly incorporating this won't be natural."

Wouldn't it be nice if other people in your life would exchange prideful evaluations for godly humility? Would you be willing to choose the path of humility?

How would you know if humility is becoming more central in your thinking? (For instance, "I'd let God judge my dad, and I'd stay out of the loop," or "As I sense former friends judging me I'd accept my limited ability to control their thoughts.")

What options do you have as you realize your wrongdoer might never incorporate humility in a way that would promote healing? (For instance, "Rather than remaining angry, I'd feel sad for that person," or "In my prayers I'd release that person's problems to God.")

God Is Sovereign

As you concentrate on the task of forgiveness, it is natural for your thoughts to gravitate toward God. Specifically, you may be challenged to determine if you really believe what you have been taught about God's acceptance of you and about His guidance over you. Brokenness in relationships has a way of revealing your innermost thoughts about God's intervention in your life.

Daniel told Dr. Minirth, "Here I am in my mid-forties, and I'm having to examine things I've never given a second thought to before. What I mean is, I'm not used to feeling like a failure. I haven't gotten divorced like a lot of my contemporaries, but my wife's trust in me is at an all-time low. My kids aren't on drugs, yet they're leery about me. My parents aren't dying of cancer, but they feel disappointed in me. I haven't been kicked out of church, but I feel the eyes of judgment on me every time I walk through its doors. I hate being branded a loser!"

How about you? What personal doubts have you had because of the judgments others hold against you? (For instance, "I feel my ex-husband is wrong in saying I was a bad wife, yet I wonder if anyone will ever want me again," or "My church's rejection of me makes me wonder if God has given up on me too.")

_____

_____

_____

Dr. Minirth empathized, "In the past, you drew strength from your Christian convictions. I'm guessing that you are not feeling sure that God does not judge you as humans do."

"Well, yeah! I mean, if everyone important in my world has judged me to be a misfit, it kinda makes me wonder whether God doesn't agree. Maybe I've just been kidding myself all these years. Maybe I'm really the manipulator everyone seems to say I am."

Notice how Daniel's struggles with human judgment caused him to struggle with God. Then notice how his diminished faith also hindered his ability to forgive.

In what ways have you had similar problems? How has your understanding of God been distorted by your painful experiences with humans? (For instance, "My church friends seem offended by my emotional frailties, so I guess God is too.")

_____

_____

_____

"There's one huge thought I want you to cling to, Daniel." Daniel was all ears as Dr. Minirth spoke. "God is completely different from humans. Our ways are not His ways. Don't make the mistake of letting human frailties influence your understanding of God's nature. He's bigger than any human, and He's certainly big enough to handle your problems."

In His sovereignty, God knew humans would disappoint and mistreat one another. He also knew that He would maintain standards separate from those of humans. One of those standards is His refusal to condemn anyone belonging to His family. The anguish of Romans chapter 7 is familiar to many. The apostle Paul bemoans how he cannot be what he wants to be, but he falls into patterns he desperately wishes to avoid. But Romans chapter 8 begins with the declaration that there is no condemnation for those who are in Christ. That great chapter ends with the pronouncement that nothing can separate us from His love.

Long-suffering, kindness, grace, and mercy—these are part of God's sovereign character. No act of humanity can change that. He is separate and distinct from human mannerisms.

Now let's use some logic at this point. If fallible, self-serving humans choose to judge you while our sovereign loving God chooses not to judge you, to whom will you hand your emotional stability? This was the question Dr. Minirth posed to Daniel.

"I know what the correct answer is. I should let God be my judge, not humans. But practically, how do I do this?"

"Knowing God's character is difficult because He cannot be seen or touched or heard," said Dr. Minirth. "You need to begin by recognizing the truth about what you *can* see. You have witnessed how humans can be terribly erratic in their pronouncements of judgment, so it is practical to say they're not very steady representatives of God. There is no need for you to let their pronouncements have the power of God over you."

"So you're suggesting that I should see God as being on an altogether different plane, meaning I can think of Him as the accepting God the Bible describes Him to be?"

"That's exactly right. See Him as very *separate*. Don't let yourself get dragged down by humans who may mean well but who live counter to the biblical teaching to let God alone be judge."

"That makes sense. I just wish I could easily keep that thought in my mind. That's the hard part."

"There was only one person who truly represented God perfectly," said Dr. Minirth, "and that of course was Jesus Christ. I want you to examine His style of dealing with people so you can get a good idea of God's style. I hope you can see how He stands out from the regular crowd."

Think back on many of the stories you have known about Jesus, giving special attention to the moments when He had opportunities to be judgmental. Whether He encountered people with moral problems, with shady reputations, with illnesses, or with confusion, how judgmental was He? Thankfully, He did not approach troubled people in the same manner as most people do. He accepted, encouraged, healed, forgave, loved, and nurtured. Do you know that Jesus?

Daniel revealed a problem common to many, "I'm very familiar with the stories about Jesus' loving ways, and I like hearing them again and again. My problem is that I don't know enough people, Christians included, who think as Jesus thought."

Have you ever had this problem? In what way have you felt that Christians misrepresent Christ's ways? (For instance, "Ever since my divorce I've felt like an outcast in some people's eyes," or "If I told people about my bitterness toward my father, they'd want me to fix it and move on.")

_____

_____

_____

Humans are, indeed, given the responsibility to represent God to others (see Acts 1:8 as a reference). But when humans fail, be willing to view God separately. Make Him your model, and Him alone.

To relate with our sovereign God as distinct from humans, you will need to operate with independence of thought, and that may not always be easy. For instance, Daniel had previously filtered his Christian convictions through his wife and his parents. "They were the ones who constantly inspired me to lean on God," he explained.

But when Daniel started having problems, he felt judged by them, meaning he felt judged by God.

"This has proved one major point," Dr. Minirth reflected. "You'll need to approach God based on your *separate* understanding of Him rather than on how your family may interpret Him to you."

Human Judges Are Without Understanding

As the apostle Paul taught the Corinthian church about God's character, he explained that people who compare or class or commend themselves in comparison with one another "are not wise" (see 2 Cor. 10:12). The same can be said today. Realize that the prevalent attitude of sizing up one another based on performance is reflective of a shallow understanding of God.

Without judging, describe some circumstances you have seen in which others have shown a lack of understanding regarding God's nonjudgmental spirit. (For instance, "When a friend had an affair I noticed that no one took the time to try to understand the causes; condemnation was readily spoken," or "Upon hearing of my conflict with my extended family, a friend expressed dismay because she's never had the same problems with her family.")

_____

_____

_____

In your opinion, what is shallow about such treatment? (For instance, "The whole perspective wasn't examined," or "The judgmental person is trying to make *himself* feel comfortable."

_____

_____

_____

How can you know if you are choosing to avoid this way of thinking? (For instance, "I'll cease defending myself" or "I'll quit being so bitter" or "I'm more committed than ever to giving away acceptance to those who need it.")

_____

_____

_____

You have permission to declare human judgments null and void. They have no power over you unless you allow it. We are not suggesting that you proceed with a closed mind whenever anyone tells you how they feel about you, but we are suggesting that you can recognize a judging spirit, and you can choose not to become entangled in nonproductive struggles with it.

Be Committed to Genuineness

When you come under judgment, it is easy to withdraw or cover up. Knowing others are warily examining you, it is tempting to put on false pretenses in an effort to minimize judgments. For instance, Daniel admitted he felt that he had to be on his best behavior when in the presence of his in-laws. "They've got the idea that I'm a self-centered lush who is bent on pleasing myself. They don't see that I've still got some good qualities."

"So how do you act when you're around them?"

"Oh, I'm *very* conscientious. I try to put on my best behavior because I *sure* don't need any more judgment than what I've already received."

"And how does that affect your efforts to forgive them?"

Daniel grinned slightly because he saw where Dr. Minirth was going with his questions. "I resent them all the more."

Has this ever happened to you? When have you tried to appease your judges with extra good behavior? (For instance, "Around my

Bible study friends I try to project a 'together' front even though I don't feel very together.")

_____

_____

_____

How does this hinder your ability to forgive? (For instance, "I can't forgive because I'm secretly bearing grudges.")

_____

_____

_____

As you determine that humans have no right to judge, our hope for you is that you will allow yourself to be just what you are, a mixture of pluses and minuses. It is our desire that you would always be in a growth mode, responding to difficulties with a fair-minded explanation of your lifestyle and your relationships. In circumstances in which you need to apologize or seek forgiveness, do so. Be mature enough to admit where you've gone wrong and where you can make constructive corrections.

Remember that you are very unlikely to act in ways that will cause the judges to stop judging. So don't assume you have to jump through someone else's hoops. Live for God and let that be enough.

Daniel shook his head as he thought about letting Daniel be Daniel. "Once again, easier said than done. I've got an army of people who are watching my every move just waiting for me to fall. It's hard to be nonchalant when you've got so many people looking judgmentally at you."

"I'm operating on a simple truth," said Dr. Minirth. "You're not going to be very successful or content if you try to be anything other than what you are. Any effort to appease judges just for the sake of appeasing will fall short. In the long run, you need to be who you are, period."

Together, Daniel and Dr. Minirth devised a plan for how Daniel should act around his skeptics, and the plan was anchored in a commitment to *genuineness*. For instance, if he was feeling uncertain in his relationship with his wife, Belinda, he would talk with her about it rather than withdrawing as he had in previous years. When with his parents, he'd try less stringently to say all the things he felt they wanted to hear. Instead, he'd relax and let them come to terms with their feelings about him in their own timing. The rule of thumb he adopted was: Don't act in any outward way that is inconsistent with your inward feelings. Be real!

And you? How could you establish more genuineness in your relations with people who judge you? (For instance, "I don't need to convince my spouse that I'm going to be the perfect Christian. Sometimes I will be less than perfect and that's okay," or "I'll not act overly friendly to my stepdad since he knows it's fake when I do.")

_____

_____

_____

As you step away from others' judgments, or you choose not to judge in return, you can then be free to make your choices based on what you believe rather than on what you think others expect. Only then can your choice to forgive feel natural and unforced.

In the meantime, as you disconnect from the judgments of others, you are more capable of connecting with God. Live with the objective of pleasing Him, not human judges.

Your task of becoming separate from judgments is made easier when you allow yourself to be honest regarding your feelings of loss. How are you in that category? We will explore that element of forgiving in the next chapter.

7

Managing Your Grief

Step 7. Allow yourself permission to grieve.

As Charlotte sat across from Dr. Carter he had an increasingly uneasy feeling about the way she was describing her predicament. About two months prior she had learned of an affair involving her husband, Gordon, and his administrative assistant. Charlotte had always known that Gordon was a flirt; in fact, she had kidded him about it many times. "I don't want you making any new girlfriends when you go to that convention," she might say. She knew he was an extrovert, but she said that she had always trusted him. He was good to her and provided a comfortable living for them both.

She sought counseling, not because she felt particularly troubled, but because a relative had told her that when your spouse has an affair, that's a big enough problem to warrant an expert's attention. So here she was, sitting in front of the good doctor willing to do whatever you're supposed to do when you go to counseling. If nothing else, this would be a novel experience for her.

After giving sketchy details of the husband's affair (supposedly it was a onetime event and nothing like this had happened before), she looked confidently at Dr. Carter and said, "I'm really doing fine because I forgave Gordy as soon as he told me about the problem. I'm not the type to hold grudges, so the only reason I'm here is just to let you check things out to make sure I'm okay."

With one visit under her belt, Charlotte opted out of counseling, certain that her problems were over. Little did she realize that they were just beginning.

Two years later Dr. Carter received a call from Charlotte. Yes, he remembered meeting her before. Yes, he had wondered how things were going. No, he didn't realize that she was now divorced. The two set up an appointment time, and this time the atmosphere was entirely different.

For starters, Charlotte, usually a perky and well-dressed young woman, looked as if she had aged ten years. Her face was drawn, eyes baggy, posture stooped. She'd been through the wringer. Gone was the confidence that seemed to show so naturally. Now she was the picture of uncertainty and despair. Her story was sad, yet it did not catch the doctor off guard because it seemed so predictable.

"You're probably going to think I'm the biggest fool who ever lived," Charlotte began. "I remember leaving your office before, assuming I had no real problems to tackle. I'm an optimist by nature, and I didn't want to have to sit in here talking about things that might get me down. But a year ago my world collapsed because I learned that Gordon hadn't had just that one overnight affair. The other woman called me and said they'd been together for over two years, and he had promised several times that he was going to leave me in order to marry her. But then *she* discovered yet another woman he was seeing on the side, and after doing some investigating she learned that this had been a way of life for him for years." She began sobbing as the ugliness of it all came back to her.

Shaking his head gently Dr. Carter spoke, "I'm so sorry to hear about this, Charlotte. I can only imagine how topsy-turvy your life has been since that call."

"It's been awful! When I told Gordy about the call he denied every word of it, but deep down I realized what she had told me was true. And he knew that I knew this. He began acting mean and hateful and in a week's time he'd hired an attorney to get the divorce papers filed. He gave me practically everything we had accumulated, but it turned out to be a lot less than I thought it was. I'm back working for the first time in twenty years, and I hate it."

"Do you remember telling me two years ago how you had forgiven Gordon for his affair?" She nodded through her tears as Dr. Carter spoke. "How about now? Do you still feel the same way?"

"I'm not sure. I don't know how I feel or what I'm supposed to feel. I'll tell you one thing, though, that I'm determined about. I don't want Gordon or anyone else to know how hurt I am. I've got to press on without letting my problems get the best of me."

What was Charlotte's problem? The uneasy feeling that Dr. Carter had felt in their first visit stemmed from the realization that she was not allowing herself to grieve for a very difficult situation. While he applauded her intent to rise above her circumstances, Dr. Carter realized she was attempting to be superhuman, as if she didn't have to feel the pain associated with severe disappointment. She had quickly determined to forgive, but her effort proved shallow because it had bypassed normal grief.

Has this ever happened to you? Have you ever been so eager to put distasteful experiences behind that you've not allowed yourself permission to grieve? When have you felt similarly compelled to brush away feelings of loss in order to get on with life? (For instance, "I don't want to have to dwell on the negatives associated

123

with my past problems with my father, so I just don't think about them.")

_____

_____

_____

While your desire is perfectly understandable, you may be in denial about your circumstances. That is, you may be operating on the assumption that the sooner you can pronounce forgiveness, the less you'll have to deal with the lingering effects of the wrongful deed. In truth, however, this reasoning only *increases* your emotional healing time since you are only storing up emotions that grow more intense and more negative with time. Reality has a way of catching up with people in denial, and when it does, watch out!

We have already examined how forgiveness cannot proceed when you suppress your anger. The same can be said about suppressing or avoiding feelings of grief. Before you can truly release a person who has wronged you, you will need to admit the extent of your sadness. Are you willing to do this?

Defining Grief

Grief can be defined as the emotion of loss associated with the anguish or sorrow caused by a negative event. While we most commonly associate grief with death, it is a natural reaction to any loss such as the loss of a friendship or the loss of innocence in a relationship that should have been safe. It follows the loss of a marriage, a job, a long-term relationship. It is experienced when dreams collapse or you are forced to admit difficult truths about someone you had trusted.

Each time you feel a loss you are dealing with a death of sorts. For instance, not only was Charlotte hurting because of the death of a marriage, but to a great degree her ability to trust a man had died too.

What "death" experience do you associate with the wrongs you have experienced? (For instance, "I feel that my relationship with my sister is dead," or "I couldn't let my former friend know that she made me hurt as badly as I did.")

_____

_____

_____

Honesty about what you feel is an essential ingredient to the forgiveness process. Not only is it okay to live in sorrow or remorse, if you have been wronged it is necessary to let your feelings be known.

Dr. Carter talked with Charlotte about their first visit. "I very distinctly remember that I felt you were too ready to pronounce forgiveness when you learned of Gordon's affair. Not that I wanted you to cling to grudges, but I sensed you didn't want to be bothered by examining uncomfortable emotions, so you chose to be rid of them by readily declaring that you'd forgiven him."

"You're not the only one who has said that. I had several friends who were furious at Gordon. They later told me that they'd been uncomfortable with his flirtations for a long time. I guess I was just too easygoing to be alarmed, but, boy, were they right on target!"

Charlotte's current intense emotions had been made more difficult by the fact that she had not been honest with herself about a truly sad set of circumstances.

To get an understanding of the nature of grief, examine the following list of traits that typically accompany this emotion. Check the ones that apply to your circumstances:

__ A sense of hopelessness that does not easily fade.
__ Social withdrawal—you don't want to be bothered.
__ The loss of joy.
__ Lack of enthusiasm regarding someone else's good fortune.
__ Feeling distant from God, wondering if He is really there.
__ Feeling physically as well as emotionally drained.

125

__ Difficulty in cheering up.
__ Pessimism about the future.
__ Feeling as if your life contains "unfinished business."
__ Sad mood more prominent than normal.
__ Reminiscing about the past more than usual.
__ Feelings of hurt or emotional pain that do not readily go away.

This list of characteristics is by no means an exhaustive list detailing grief, but it can give you a good idea of what is included in grief reactions. If you have been on the receiving end of wrong behavior, it would be strange if you did *not* respond to some of these items. Most people who need to forgive someone else can relate to at least six or more of these traits. If you fall into this category, you are very normal. Your task is not necessarily to get rid of your grief but to understand it so you can remain balanced as you seek to forgive.

What traits or behaviors have you experienced as part of your grief? (For instance, "I've withdrawn from my friends ever since I lost my job," or "I've been depressed because of my lost relationship with my best friend.")

_____

_____

_____

As Dr. Carter talked with Charlotte she admitted, "Two years ago I had every reason to grieve about the loss of innocence that had come upon my marriage, but I was afraid to give in to my feelings."

"So you were kidding yourself when you jumped so quickly at the choice to just forgive," the doctor reflected. "I guess you thought the pain would go away if you could just convince yourself that you didn't hurt as badly as you did."

"I wouldn't have said it like that back then, but yeah, you're right. I wanted to brush the grief aside as quickly as possible. I think, though, that it set me up to take the news of his multiple affairs much more poorly. I've never liked looking bad news right in the face."

A History of Running from Grief

People like Charlotte who minimize their true grief usually have a history of sweeping hard emotions under the rug. Too commonly they tell themselves how they will easily choose forgiveness when, in fact, they are really minimizing their pain with a form of well-intended dishonesty.

As Dr. Carter got to know Charlotte better, he began probing into her personal background, suspicious that she might have a history of minimizing pain. She had already told him that her family did not process emotions well and that her father in particular was very hard on her and her sisters. In one discussion she admitted, "Several times when I was thirteen or fourteen my older brother tried to sexually molest me. He was a bully anyway, and I hated being around him. When he'd mess with me sexually I'd feel even more angry at him."

"Did you ever blow the whistle on him? Did you bring your parents in on the problem?"

"Yes, but it just backfired. My mom just told me not to be alone with him, and I actually think my dad thought the whole thing was kinda funny. It slowed my brother down, knowing that I had said something about it, but he was still mean to me whenever he got the chance."

Dr. Carter asked Charlotte to consider what a more ideal relationship would have been like with her brother. It would not have been out of the ordinary for her to want her big brother to be a protector, a guide, a friend. That's what God's design would have called for. But instead he became an adversary, a tormentor. "That's a loss you endured, something to be genuinely grieved."

"Well, I didn't grieve about my problems then because no one allowed me the luxury of exploring how I felt. It was easier to just move on and try not to let it get me down."

That last sentence perfectly summarized Charlotte's approach to her grief. Move on. It is this attitude that often causes people to forgive too quickly. Fearful that their grief will be considered insignificant, they try to wrap it up ASAP.

In what ways have you been tempted to resolve your grief too quickly? (For instance, "I broke up with a longtime boyfriend and tried to compensate by staying busy with other friends," or "I've not wanted to admit how betrayed I felt over past abuse.")

_____

_____

_____

As you look back on your overeagerness to resolve grief, how were you just kidding yourself about the seriousness of your loss? (For instance, "I told myself I didn't need that friendship anyway when, in fact, I really did.")

_____

_____

_____

In your early developmental years how did you learn to minimize feelings of loss? (For instance, "I was specifically told no one wanted to hear about my problems," or "I felt too ashamed to tell anyone about my problems, so I just didn't.")

_____

_____

_____

It is completely understandable that you would prefer not to dwell on your feelings of loss, and it is not our intent to encourage you to go to the opposite extreme of camping out in your pain. We do want you to be aware, though, that you need to forgive for the right reasons. Forgiveness for the purpose of hurrying past your loss is poor motivation because it involves denial. It is ultimately dishonest. So just as you need permission to feel anger, you need permission to admit the depth of feelings of loss and sadness before you can find true forgiveness.

Before we examine ways to resolve your grief, first examine the potential adjustments you may need to make in the way you experience grief.

- Will you be able to admit how hurt you have felt without making excuses for the wrongdoer?

- Can you recognize *openly* the loss you have experienced?

- Will you allow trusted friends to know the extent of your loss?

- Before rushing to rebuild your dreams, will you allow a season of time to pass so you can find a broader perspective on what your adjustments will be?

- If someone asks you, "How's it going?" can you be honest?

- Can you let a trusted friend console you without feeling that you've got to be strong?

As you consider adjustments you could make in order to be able to grieve, what changes might be in order for you? (For instance, "I don't need to smile as much as I tell myself I should," or "I'd have to admit that it's normal to feel the loss that I feel; it doesn't mean I'm a weakling.")

The Grief Process

At first, Charlotte balked when Dr. Carter suggested she admit more openly how she felt at a point of great loss. "I've always preached that you should handle adversity with a positive attitude," she explained. "What you're suggesting doesn't sound all that positive."

"I'm all for positive attitudes," he replied. "If you'll recall two years ago, your overeagerness to forgive was done for the purpose of remaining positive, but you were really just kidding yourself. That made your current problems all the more difficult to accept. I'm hoping that your open admission of loss will actually help you find a more permanent and more positive ability to forgive. Even if it means that you take a little more time up front to grieve, in the long run you'll be better off."

When we suggest that you give yourself permission to grieve, exactly what do we mean? Let's look at five major elements of the grief process.

1. Be Mournful About Sin

Sin is an old-fashioned word that has become unpopular with some people who don't like to look squarely at wrongdoing as it really is. But try as hard as we can, we cannot come up with a more appropriate word to describe much of the behavior that has brought pain upon our patients. Simply defined, *sin* is the choice to live outside God's design for successful living.

Think of the standards designed by God for the purpose of bringing contentment to His people. The Bible instructs us to be loving, kind, humble, respectful, considerate, caring, giving. Our list could be very long, but you get the idea. God's intent is for His creation to live freely within such guidelines.

Now, think about the circumstances you have had to endure. How closely did they match the design laid out by God? Our guess is that your pain was the direct result of someone living opposed to God's design. You've been subjected to rejection or scorn or judgment or manipulation. In short, you have experienced the disabling power of sin.

As you consider the wrongs done against you, what sinful elements were at the core? (For instance, "It was sinful when my father was so rejecting," or "My husband's chronic withdrawal from me was because of selfishness, which is sin.")

_____

_____

_____

When we call sin by its name, we are not encouraging judgments, merely descriptions. Just as others have sinned against you, you also have sinned in some way, meaning you have no right to judge. Our purpose is not to be haughty in regarding others' misdeeds, but to be honest about the ugliness of it.

Do you let yourself mourn over the presence of sin in your world? Jesus Himself cried in anguish as He overlooked Jerusalem because He agonized over the ill effects of sin. You, too, may shake your head in holy disgust as you consider the many choices made by people living outside God's will.

Dr. Carter told Charlotte, "On that first occasion when I met you and I saw how upbeat you were as you described your quick decision to forgive Gordon's adultery, I had the uneasy sense that you didn't want to tarry long on the idea that something very wrong had come into your life."

"Well, your senses were pretty accurate. I *didn't* want to look at the sinfulness of what had happened. I guess I'm just not a very judgmental person."

"I'm not talking about being judgmental. I'm referring instead to the normalcy of feeling downright sadness for something in your life that had gone wrong. It's okay and necessary to mourn at a time like that."

As they discussed Charlotte's reluctance to mourn sin, Dr. Carter introduced an idea related to her past. "One of the most common trends I see in people who were sexually abused is the tendency to withhold normal emotional reactions to blatant wrong. As a girl trying to figure out how to handle your brother's abuse, you probably concluded that it wasn't safe to expose how you really felt."

"That's an understatement! If I ever told on him, he'd make my life more miserable than ever. Even though he stopped sexually abusing me when our parents found out about it, he made a point to keep me on edge whenever the mood struck him. I tried to just block out my feelings about him because it seemed to hurt less when I'd act disinterested."

"I know you were merely trying to protect yourself at that point in your life, and you certainly can't be faulted for doing the best you knew to do. What I'm wanting you to see now is that you no longer have to deny your feelings in the face of pain. Sin hurts! You're not going to bring damage upon yourself by openly declaring that you strongly dislike sin."

If you were to attend the funeral of a close friend or relative, it would be abnormal if you did not mourn that person's passing. In the same sense, allow yourself to express sadness in the wake of wrongdoing. Even if substantial time has passed since the wrong deed, your mourning can be appropriate just as it is appropriate in the months and years after a loved one's death.

If you allowed yourself to mourn the sinfulness of your losses, how would you be affected? (For instance, "I wouldn't apologize for the hurt that my broken relationship has caused," or "I'd admit more honestly that I feel cheated by my friend's rejection.")

_____

_____

_____

_____

2. Make Room for Loneliness

As Dr. Carter and Charlotte discussed her tendency to minimize her grief, they discussed how she was afraid of loneliness. A major factor in forgiving Gordon too quickly was her fear of being abandoned. In retrospect, she realized that she had reasoned, "If I don't forgive him right away, he'll leave me, I'll be all alone, and then my world would *really* collapse."

The doctor explained, "You were using an all-or-nothing thinking style. You saw a very high potential for separation from Gordon if you admitted the depth of your grief, so you concluded that the isolation would be too devastating to handle."

"Well, isolation *is* devastating! I don't like it one bit."

"I don't like it either, so I'm not discounting your distaste for it. What I am suggesting is that you not assume that some loneliness will completely ruin your life. When you grieve, sometimes you feel that no one else can possibly understand what you feel. There's a sense of solitude that you can't avoid. By being less threatened by that solitude, though, you can at least keep the emptiness from being completely overwhelming. By making some allowance for its presence you are also assuming that you have the strength to persevere."

When you are in a position to forgive it is because a major gap has opened between yourself and someone who had a significant role in your life. You had hoped for a feeling of connectedness, but instead you felt disconnected. Loneliness is an unfortunate, but inevitable, by-product of wrongdoing.

In what ways has your broken experience caused you to feel lonely? (For instance, "When I'm with friends I don't feel I can discuss the pain caused by my rift with my best friend," or "Everyone else seems to have a normal life, so I feel isolated knowing that my life is upside-down.")

_____

_____

_____

How might you try to avoid or deny your feelings of loneliness? (For instance, "I push myself to keep a very busy schedule," or "I won't admit to anyone that I feel empty.")

_____

_____

_____

Do yourself a favor. Allow yourself to grieve over the fact that gaps exist in your life. There are several things that might help you openly expose and explore this aspect of your grief.

- If possible, talk with someone about your lonely feelings, explaining how you've felt isolated because of your experiences. You'll not be doing this for the purpose of finding immediate solutions to your problems but for the purpose of being honest.

- Spend time alone. This may not be an enjoyable experience, yet you need time to let your sad feelings come forward. Admit to yourself that you feel sad and if tears flow, let them flow.

- Write about your feelings. Perhaps you could write a letter to the person who has disappointed you, detailing how dashed hopes have created sadness. You might also keep a journal detailing how your days are impacted by your emotional highs and lows.

• Don't assume you have to be upbeat at all times in public. While you won't necessarily want to make a spectacle of your sadness, don't be phony. It's okay at times to let folks know that things are less than ideal for you.

By suggesting that you allow yourself to feel your loneliness, we are operating on a basic belief that the failure to be real regarding your grief will *strengthen* grief's hold on you.

What adjustment might you make as you allow this aspect of grief to run its course? (For instance, "I need to trim my schedule, allowing for some time of quiet reflection," or "I need to let family and friends know that sometimes I'm not going to be my bubbly self.")

_____

_____

_____

3. Say Good-Bye to Some Ideals

A regular ingredient in grief-producing situations is poor treatment. You don't feel grief in the presence of kindness, acceptance, consideration, or encouragement. It is degradation, judgment, rudeness, or insults that produce grief.

Intellectually you probably have no difficulty admitting this reality, but emotionally, well, that's a different story. As you choose to forgive, you are also choosing to set aside the hope for some ideal circumstances, and that is not an emotionally pleasing task.

For instance, when Charlotte began dating she had the ideal notion that she could find a man who would treat her far better than her abusive brother had. In the early years Gordon was a charmer who gave her every reason to believe that he could satisfy her romantic dreams. When she first learned of his sexual indiscretion she desperately did not want to give up her dream, so she forgave quickly while tentatively holding on to the ideal that he would still be her white knight. Later, when she learned the full truth about the depth of his problems, she still tried to deny how bad the situation was.

As long as she clung to unrealistic ideals, she remained bound by her pain. Forgiveness required her to set aside her illusions and openly recognize unwanted reality.

What ideals have you not wanted to let go of? (For instance, "I just can't accept that my father could be such an indecent man," or "I don't like thinking that my Christian friends can be so hard-headed in their opinions; they should be full of grace.")

_____

_____

_____

What hard realities will you need to accept as part of your grief and loss? (For instance, "My mother seems committed to being selfish," or "Friends can turn on you.")

_____

_____

_____

How can you know if you are setting aside unrealistic ideals and living within reality? Listed here are some common indicators that may show whether you are handling grief realistically.

- You will not speculate endlessly about what caused your wrong-doer to act as he or she did.

- You will keep balance in your conversations about your problems. When appropriate, you'll talk about your pain, yet you'll not discuss it obsessively.

- You will not yearn for a new set of idealistic conditions to pull you out of your pain.

- You will drop phrases such as "I just can't believe . . ."

- Even as you allow yourself to feel sad, you will also hold on to the belief that you can eventually move forward.

By suggesting that you say good-bye to some ideals, we are not saying you should cease having dreams or lofty goals. We are saying, though, that you must factor in the truth that life can and does disappoint.

4. Don't Be Ashamed to Hurt

One of Charlotte's original problems was embarrassment about her painful circumstances. Her first reaction to the news of Gordon's affair was, "What will people think?" When her marriage came to an end, her embarrassment doubled. *Now I'm going to look like a failure*, she frequently thought.

The inability to forgive often exists in direct proportion to the tendency to hold on to unnecessary shame or embarrassment. Shame causes you to be phony, and this inhibits you from being honest with others about your pain. More important, it keeps you from being honest with yourself.

Consider the circumstances that require your forgiveness. What shame or embarrassment do you carry because of it? (For instance, "I'm embarrassed that my friends have been so cold toward me," or "I don't want anyone to know how my spouse mistreats me. I'd feel as though it's a poor reflection upon me.")

———————————————————

———————————————————

———————————————————

How does holding on to shame slow your grieving process? (For instance, "I can't let myself grieve as long as I'm keeping up such a strong guard," or "I can't let on that I'm dying inside.")

Let yourself be honest about the hurt you feel. If you suffered a broken leg no one would think ill of you if you said you were in pain. Perhaps others won't demonstrate the same understanding of your emotional pain, but that is almost always caused by their general discomfort with uneasy emotions. In no way should you take on others' discomfort to the extent that you deny your legitimate hurt.

Dr. Carter asked Charlotte, "Let's just be as logical as we can. You attempted to be a good wife. You were faithful. You were open to improvements. But in spite of that, Gordon chose to pursue a lifestyle that brought your marriage to an end. Can you see that it would be strange if you *didn't* hurt?"

"Well, since you put it that way, I guess I can't argue with what you're saying."

"I'm only suggesting that you not carry embarrassment or shame for a very normal reaction."

What is normal about the hurt you have felt? (For instance, "It's normal to be hurt after the backstabbing I've experienced," or "I'm normal to wish my relationship with my daughter could have been mended.")

How can you help yourself by dropping shame that might be associated with your hurt? (For instance, "I need to remind myself that in spite of my mistakes in my marriage, I'm willing to grow," or "I can stop justifying my past so powerfully.")

Shame belongs only in incidents in which no repentance or remorse is registered. If you know yourself to be conscientious and growing, shame has no place in your life.

5. Commit to an End to Your Grief

When you have experienced a trauma or a major letdown, your grief will know some very intense moments. As time progresses, you will still have recurrences of your sadness, but they will probably spread out over time.

Have you ever experienced surgery? If you have, you know that it is followed by a period of intense pain, then by a progressively diminishing experience of pain. Your pain may not go away completely, yet it is expected that the intense experience of it will eventually subside. The same can be said for the pain associated with the circumstances requiring forgiveness.

While you may not feel that relief is yet in sight for your pain, what future relief might you reasonably hope for? (For instance, "As I get used to life without my former best friend, it's reasonable to assume that new friends will come into my life.")

The inability to forgive is often driven by pessimism that life will never progress beyond the current grief. For instance, Charlotte once said, "My life will never be the same. I'm ruined!"

Dr. Carter responded, "I can agree with the first half of what you said, but the second half is an overstatement. You *will* reach a time when life doesn't seem like a complete heap of ruins."

"I know that's true, but right now I just don't feel it's true."

Knowing and feeling are two separate matters. Be sure your emotions don't completely overwhelm the facts. In order to set your sights on the end to your grief, certain steps can be followed.

- When a friend offers words of comfort or consolation, receive them. You may feel like discounting them for the time being; nonetheless, be thankful for encouragement.

- Be willing to talk with someone who has encountered similar problems. You'll learn that your doubts are normal, and you'll learn that time can provide perspective and healing.

- Stay away from all-or-nothing statements. (For instance, "I'll *never* trust a friend again.") This only cements you in pessimism and keeps you from entertaining healing experiences in the future.

- Keep in touch with routine matters. Though your grief may legitimately cause you to be more inhibited, don't go to such an extreme that you lose touch with *some* normal activities.

- Don't push yourself to forgive right away, but assume you will do so when the timing is right. Your expectation of healing will help generate realistic hope.

Balance is required in the grieving process. On one hand, you will need to let it be in you. On the other hand, you can know that your loss does not represent the sum total of your life's experiences.

8

Confrontations

Step 8. Confront the injuring party if appropriate.

So far we have discussed the personal adjustments you can make as you choose forgiveness in your circumstance. Sometimes, though, you may be unable to proceed in forgiving until you make an effort to explain to the wrongdoer changes he or she could make. In most cases, that is a very difficult task. We have counseled numerous people who have developed excellent insights into their emotions but have been unable to move forward because the wrongdoer persists in harmful patterns. In some cases, forgiveness can be accomplished without direct involvement with the other party, but in many cases forgiveness is impossible until an open confrontation is made.

Daniel, the alcoholic whose problems prompted an onslaught of judgment from his extended family, had made great strides in coming to terms with his history of poor emotional management. In both his individual counseling and his 12-Step support group he had been

141

challenged to take responsibility for his past mistakes by altering his lifestyle habits. As he made his personal adjustments it became increasingly clear that he had been in a very unhealthy family system.

"One thing has become abundantly clear," he explained to Dr. Minirth. "Not only have I spent my entire life avoiding emotional issues, but the rest of my family is in the same rut. It's like we have a quiet, unspoken commitment to sidestep any problem that is emotionally charged. No wonder we're not getting along with one another!"

"What evidence do you see that this is a familywide problem?"

"Do you remember when I told you that years ago my dad had a girlfriend on the side, and I was the only one who knew about it?" The doctor nodded as Daniel continued. "I'm realizing that he's got lots of secret chambers in his life. In many respects he's a mystery man because I'm not sure that his public image matches what he is really like in his private moments. And the same goes for my mother. She had a bad back in years past and got hooked on prescription pain relievers. I think she takes pills now because they just numb her to her *emotional* pain. She won't deal openly with *any* of her hurts."

"Have you talked with them about these observations?"

"Well, a couple of times I tried to bring up the subject with my dad, but he's not very receptive to personal communication. He never asks about my treatment because he seems embarrassed that a son of his would actually need psychological counseling."

Then, speaking with concern, Daniel explained, "My relationship with my parents is going downhill fast. When I began admitting the problems Belinda and I have faced during the last several years, they became increasingly critical and negative. What's worse, they've been buddying up with my son, Brian, like they're trying to turn him against me."

"In what way?"

"He's a junior in college now, and I think he's been turning things around in his life for the better. For example, I've talked with him about how alcohol started getting a foothold in my life when I was about his age, and we've had several excellent discussions about his beliefs and his choices."

"That sounds *very* encouraging," said Dr. Minirth. "You're sure to feel like your problems haven't been a complete waste if you can use them to have productive discussions with Brian."

"But there's a hitch in all this," Daniel explained. "My son's college is in the same town as my parents' home. He sees them a couple of times a month, and I can tell without even asking when they've talked to each other. He becomes more cynical. He withdraws from me. He gets moody."

"What do your parents say to him that creates this friction between you and Brian?"

"As best as I can determine, they talk with him about their disappointment in me—you know, the fact that I became an alcoholic, that I went through bankruptcy, that I've struggled in my faith. They're pessimistic by nature, and it's common for them to make remarks about negative things whenever the opportunities arise."

"Have you discussed this with your parents?"

"Well, sort of. I've told them about my counseling, and I've asked them not to say negative things to Brian, but I'm not sure any of it gets through. They just humor me and go on about their business. I don't think they understand how their critical nature is hurting my effort to positively influence Brian."

How about you? Have you ever felt your efforts to move forward have been hindered by someone who seems to be working against you? Do others seem to associate you only with your past mistakes or failures? Has this slowed your efforts to move away from your pain?

What experiences have you had with others who continue to hold you back from personal growth? (For instance, "When I'm with my brother he seems to take delight in my marriage problems," or "My friend has told me it's ridiculous that I'm not recovered from the fallout with my daughter.")

_____

_____

_____

Have you tried to say something in self-defense only to find that it didn't get through? (For instance, "I told my brother that his attitude hurt my feelings, but I'm not sure he even cared about what I said.")

_____

_____

_____

In Chapter 4 we explored how necessary it can be to establish your boundaries as you also decide to forgive. Let's add that your efforts may not come full circle until you have attempted to plainly confront the other person regarding past pain or regarding ongoing problems that perpetuate your pain. Are you up to it?

Following are some common circumstances we have encountered that required a direct confrontation. Look them over to determine whether one or more parallel your experience.

- Former friends or acquaintances speak openly and detrimentally about your past problems.

- A brother or sister continues to treat you in harsh or condescending ways.

- As you are making changes in your life, a family member or friend tries to relate in ways that would perpetuate the problematic habits.

- Others openly disown your values.

- Efforts you make to mend broken relationships are shunned.

- You have been the subject of unfair criticism.

- Manipulative behavior from family or friends persists.

- The behavior of another person clearly hinders your ability to pursue healthy relationship goals.

- Wrong information about you or someone you love is being spoken as truth.

- You have discovered evidence indicating that a friend or family member has been lying to you.

Can you relate to any of these possibilities? If you have been wronged, there is a strong likelihood that you will encounter uncomfortable aftereffects, which will then create the dilemma: Do you just ignore the problem in hopes that it will eventually pass, or do you confront it directly? Either option has its downside. Ignoring the problem can be the beginning of suppressed anger, which in turn can feed depression, anxiety, disillusionment, or rage. Confronting the problem can stir up new conflict, reexpose painful feelings, or ignite others' controlling ways.

Look back over the previous list. What circumstances in your life parallel these experiences? (For instance, "My brother speaks half-truths about me to the rest of my family," or "A coworker keeps trying to get me to go to happy hours after work even though he knows I'm trying to change my habits.")

_____

_____

_____

What are the risks of confronting the persons who are working against you? (For instance, "My brother is capable of making family gatherings miserable for everyone," or "My coworker could block advances in my career.")

_____

_____

_____

Why Confront?

As you consider the possibility of confronting a wrongdoer, first examine your motives. Why would you want to do it? What could be gained by it? What needs to be communicated?

Dr. Minirth spoke with Daniel. "It's bad enough that your parents seem unable to appreciate the efforts you're making to find new foundations for your lifestyle. I'm guessing that they feel threatened by your self-examinations because they might force them to admit some matters in their own lives that need changing. Confronting them about their resistance may be a good idea, yet there is a distinct possibility they won't receive what you have to say."

"At this point, I'm willing to take that risk. I love my mom and dad, and I want to talk about ways we can deepen our love for one another," Daniel explained. "Now, though, I've got an extra reason for confronting—Brian. I don't want them to disrupt the good thing I've got going with him. Whether they change or not, I've got to protect my relationship with him. I don't need them sabotaging me."

Let's first look at two reasons *not* to confront.

Some people confront as a means of punishment or intimidation. Perhaps they have very good reasons to say what they say, yet there is a desire to make the wrongdoer squirm in discomfort. They reason, "I've had to put up with your mistreatment, now it's your turn to be in the hot seat!" (Remember the message of Chapter 5: "Refuse to be in the inferior position and resist the desire to be superior.")

Daniel admitted, "Having a relationship with Brian is very important to my parents. Of the four grandkids they have, he's by far the most accomplished and the most likable. I've thought about keeping Brian permanently away from them just to show them that they're *not* going to manipulate my son against me." Of course, an attempt at such a power play would only escalate the battle, and eventually Brian would be the worse because of it.

Be honest. What punishing or intimidating motives might accompany your desire to confront? (For instance, "Sometimes I confront my husband just to prove he's not as righteous as he thinks he is," or "I feel like giving my former friend a dose of her own medicine.")

_____

_____

_____

A second reason not to confront is for the purpose of embarrassment. Often in cases of wrongdoing you can feel humiliated. Ask people who have suffered abuse or who have been unfairly rejected, and they will admit that a primal instinct was to plan how to respond in kind. For instance, Daniel recalled eating a meal with his extended family shortly after he initiated his treatment for alcoholism. When his brother-in-law mentioned something about a company party, Daniel's mother quipped barely audibly, "I'm glad Daniel doesn't have to go to those kinds of functions now that we know he's got a drinking problem." Daniel turned beet red as the words stung his ego.

When you've felt embarrassed you may be tempted to give back what you have received. Daniel admitted, "When mother made that comment, I wanted so badly to say something about her pain pill habit, but I didn't." Perhaps you have had similar feelings.

What feelings of embarrassment have you felt because of someone else's insensitivity? (For instance, "I've been embarrassed to attend my weekly woman's Bible class because they're all aware of the fallout I've had with one of the ladies.")

_____

_____

_____

How have you been tempted to respond by embarrassing someone in return? (For instance, "I'd like to make my dad feel what it's like to put his worst mistakes on display, as mine have been.")

_____

_____

_____

Whatever you may temporarily accomplish by embarrassing another person will soon be erased by the increase in tension it will produce in you.

There are also two good reasons to confront: (1) To establish self-respect through an improved understanding of your needs, or (2) To potentially restore (or establish) a relationship.

Confronting to Establish Self-Respect

As you forgive, you are committing to a long-term mind-set of personal wholeness. Part of that wholeness includes an abiding sense of respect toward yourself. The wrong deeds committed against you in some way robbed you of your dignity. Forgiveness is possible only as you recoup that dignity, and often this can happen only as you stand up and speak out on your own behalf.

That's what Daniel wanted to accomplish with his parents. He felt badly enough about his past because of his business and his personal failures. His parents' disdain toward him was rubbing salt into the wound. Through his counseling he had made great advances in restoring his self-respect; now he hoped to complete his task by restoring respect in the eyes of his parents. Because they were not inclined to give him credit on their own, he was justified in speaking to them in a manner that would help the process along.

"I want to encourage you," Dr. Minirth told him, "to hold your head high as you talk with your parents about your feelings. You can tell a lot about people's character by observing the way they respond to mistakes, and I think you have responded to your own mistakes in an exemplary fashion."

"Well, my intent is to ask them to respect me for my efforts, even though they may still feel disappointed in what I've done in the past. Their attitude adjustment would go a long way in helping me heal."

How about you? In what way might your confrontation represent your healthy self-respect? (For instance, "By confronting the 'other woman' I'd be illustrating that I'm not someone to be lightly discarded," or "In confronting my former friend, I'd be communicating that I don't deserve the rumors being falsely spread about me.")

_____

_____

_____

Confronting to Repair a Broken Relationship

A second reason to confront is for the repairing of a relationship. Perhaps prior to the wrongdoing you enjoyed a reasonable relationship with the one who is now at odds with you. Because of the ensuing pain you may never be able to restore the relationship to what it once was, but the confrontation may go a long way toward removing the negatives you do not want.

Daniel told Dr. Minirth, "The breakdown in my relationship with my parents has been building for some time, and right now we're at an all-time low. I don't think I'll ever have quite the trust I once had in my parents, but I don't want it to remain as bad as it is now."

Dr. Minirth reflected, "So even if you can't recoup the entire relationship, you're at least hoping you can get it back to a pleasant level."

"Well, yeah. For as long as we all are alive I'll be seeing them at holidays and such. I want to feel that I've done all I could to minimize the hurt and disappointment we've all faced."

In our counseling, we have encountered numerous circumstances that required a confrontation in order for restoration to come to a relationship. For instance:

- A woman needs to talk with a longtime friend about a major run-in over their daughters' hurt feelings. Each woman carries scars related to her own child's pain.

- A worker needs to discuss differences of opinion with a co-worker because failure to do so would perpetuate an icy chill in the office atmosphere.

- A man needs to discuss his feelings with his ex-wife about their separate lives, because he wants civility to reign when they share joint activities with their children.

- An adult son or daughter needs to explain to a parent how hurt he or she felt over past differences because their failure to talk could eventually tear the entire family apart.

What restoration goals might guide *you* as you confront the person you've been in conflict with? (For instance, "I want to explain my needs to my roommate because the lack of understanding between the two of us is creating an uncomfortable bitterness," or "I'm going to discuss family problems with my brother because I want our relationship to continue so our kids can still enjoy one another's friendship.")

_____

_____

_____

Preparing to Confront

Once you have decided that a confrontation will be made with constructive intentions, it is best to gather your thoughts carefully. Memories of the conflict-producing circumstances probably evoke strong emotions in you or the other person, meaning extra effort will be required to ensure that rationality will prevail. Don't make the mistake of going into a confrontation shooting from the hip.

In the case of Daniel's parents, they had strong emotions about his past alcoholism. Both parents had good reason for feeling as they did about this problem, but because of their emotions they were not very objective. Daniel, too, had strong emotions about their response to his alcoholism. He had been to the bottom of the barrel and now was genuinely wanting to correct his life. His parents' opinion of him was very important, and it hurt him greatly to be condemned by them. He, too, could not be counted on to be purely objective in an off-the-cuff confrontation.

"The first thing I want to suggest," said Dr. Minirth, "is that you write a letter to your parents detailing what you feel, the factors leading up to those feelings, and what you hope to resolve with them. I want you to get your thoughts organized so you won't just ramble when you actually sit down and talk with them."

You, too, would probably benefit greatly by writing your thoughts and feelings in letter form before you confront. As you organize the letter you could include such topics as:

- A summary of the good aspects of your history with the other person.

- A *brief*, factual summary of the circumstances that produced the conflict.

- Your understanding of the legitimate aspects of the other person's perspective and feelings.

- A description of your feelings of hurt or anger or confusion, without accusations.

- A description of the constructive changes you would like to see in your relationship.

- A description of the adjustments you will make (if necessary) as part of the reconciliation process.

In the space below, list the general topics you would need to include in your own letter. (For instance, "I'd include my memories of good times with my dad, how I came to feel hurt by him, the struggle the conflict produced in me, the changes in communication I'd like to see between us, and my plans for the future of our relationship.")

_____

_____

_____

Later, when Daniel spoke with Dr. Minirth, he admitted, "I had no idea my letter would be so hard to produce. I've rehearsed a speech dozens of times as I've thought about things I'd like to say to Mom and Dad, but now I can see those speeches contained lots of accusations. Rereading what I've written made me look carefully at my choice of words."

"I think you're seeing that confrontations need to be managed with tact and with a constructive purpose. There's no need to air out your feelings if it is virtually certain that it will make matters worse. You're dealing with a loaded subject!"

"I'll say! I probably wrote four or five drafts before I finally got things out the way I wanted."

You, like Daniel, may have to similarly struggle to pull together your thoughts and feelings in a constructive manner. As an additional suggestion, you would benefit by including an objective partner as you gather your thoughts. That partner may be a counselor, your spouse, a close friend who has been through similar experiences, or a minister. Be willing to let someone else filter your words since you are likely to be too close to the subject to be perfectly objective.

The Actual Confrontation

Once you have decided that you have constructive intentions, and once you have formulated your thoughts, it will be time to speak with the other person. We suggest that you refrain from confronting on special days (for example, Christmas Eve or the person's birthday) so the event will not be forevermore linked with the confrontation. If taking a witness or an ally with you will help, this is perfectly legitimate, though in most cases you should refrain from confronting with many people. In Daniel's case, he asked his brother to accompany him because he was fair-minded and he had the trust and confidence of both parents.

As you are talking with the other person, stick to the subject. Don't ramble, and don't begin chasing subjects not germane to the problem. In many cases people read the letter in its entirety as a means of staying within the purposes of the confrontation. Others have taken a notepad with reminders of the topics to be discussed. Do whatever is most likely to produce objectivity.

Daniel decided to go to his parents' home to talk about his needs and feelings. He called in advance to clear their schedule and he mentioned only that he had a serious matter he wanted to discuss. "Once I hung up the phone, I knew I was committed to following through, and it gave me strength to go on," Daniel recalled. "I was nervous, but I was also determined to follow through."

As you consider actually following through with your confrontation, what fears or concerns are most common to you? (For

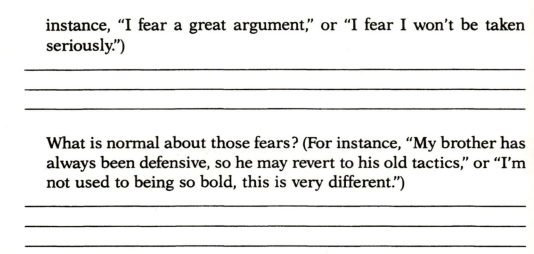

instance, "I fear a great argument," or "I fear I won't be taken seriously.")

_____

_____

_____

What is normal about those fears? (For instance, "My brother has always been defensive, so he may revert to his old tactics," or "I'm not used to being so bold, this is very different.")

_____

_____

_____

Acknowledge your anxiety, yet don't let it weigh you down. Once Daniel arrived at his parents' home, they spent a few minutes exchanging simple pleasantries; but he soon decided to dive into the subject at hand. He chose not to read his letter because he wanted the conversation to be as natural as possible, but he did refer to notes he had made.

"Mom and Dad," he began, "for the past several months there has been a strain on our relationship, and you mean too much to me to let this become permanent. I'm here to talk with you about my problems with alcoholism, your reactions to my problems, and your involvement of Brian in matters that I'd like to keep between us." He asked that they hear him out with no interruptions, then he discussed the issues in the order he had laid out on his note card.

His parents listened carefully, but as he spoke he could not get a good read on their feelings about what he was saying. He had been coached by Dr. Minirth not to get too excited in his emotions because his intent was to get them to respond to his words, not his exaggerated feelings.

As you speak to the person who has wronged you, keep one major thought in mind: Your purpose is not persuasion or salesmanship. You are in the position of conflict because you have two very different perspectives, so don't blindly assume that your confrontation will produce a suddenly new agreement. To do so would be setting yourself up for major disappointment or anger.

Speak without coercion. Let your tone of voice be unexcited, yet firm. As you speak, keep in mind how you like to be spoken to during a confrontation. You don't want to hear condescending or pleading or invalidating tones; therefore, determine that you will refrain from these.

In order to refrain from using salesmanship, what will you need to remind yourself of as you confront? (For instance, "I need to remember that this person often leads with defensiveness," or "I'll remember that I'm discussing a very touchy subject that is likely to be emotionally loaded for the other person.")

_____

_____

_____

Finish your explanation of your feelings and desires, then be quiet to allow time for absorption.

Managing a Poorly Received Confrontation

As you confront, be realistic enough to know that there is a strong likelihood that your perspective will not be well received. Don't be shocked if you do not get the desired result. If you had a high probability of agreement, you would probably not be in the position to confront in the first place.

Once Daniel finished saying everything that needed to be said, there was a moment of awkward silence. But then, his mother began crying. "I don't like being accused of trying to turn Brian against you. I'm not the divisive person you've made me out to be. You *know* I'd never deliberately hurt him or you."

His dad chimed in, "When you called to tell us you were coming,

I had an idea you would do something like this. I'm not sure I like you coming here making your mother all upset."

Immediately Daniel had a knot in his stomach, or let's say the knot that was already there grew bigger. He thought to himself, *I should have known they'd get defensive, now what?*

Put yourself in Daniel's position. Being as honest as you can, what would you do if your confrontation was met with denial or defensiveness? (For instance, "I'd become heated in my anger," or "I'd try to defend my position.")

As you encounter opposition, remember the purpose of a confrontation: to establish self-respect and to potentially restore a relationship. Notice that your purpose is *not* to convince the other person of your correctness. If that person is capable of receiving your words and feelings, consider yourself fortunate. If not, do not make it your business to force agreement.

When Daniel heard how his parents reacted to his confrontation, he wisely realized that it would be of no avail to argue. His response was simple, "It's not my intention to blame or accuse. I only felt it necessary to remind you that I have a different perspective that I'd like to be respected."

"Well, Son, if you think we're trying to poison Brian's mind, you're way off base. We're just talking with him about family problems, just like anyone else would."

"I'm not challenging your right to speak with him, I simply wanted to register my perspective."

"And another thing," his dad continued, "don't think you can continue bringing up a sore subject like this every time our family gets together. As I said, I don't want you upsetting your mother."

"I'm just communicating a perspective, that's all."

Do you realize what Daniel was doing? Each time he was given the opportunity to enter into an emotional debate (which no one would win), he sidestepped it. He had gone to his parents' house to present his thoughts and had determined beforehand that he would not succumb to the position of self-defense, nor would he take it upon himself to ramrod his position home. His neutral responses to their defensiveness kept the discussion from falling completely apart.

As you consider the possibility of a less-than-warm welcome to your confrontation, what could you do as a protection against being pulled into a greater battle? (For instance, "I would remind myself that I can consider the conversation a success if I am able to stand unwaveringly upon the truth," or "I will determine that it's not necessary to enter into a debate.")

_____

_____

_____

Listening to Counter-Confrontations

Before going to his parents' house Daniel had decided that "turnabout is fair play." He wanted to be heard as he spoke his feelings. If his parents had thoughts or feelings to express it would only be fair to hear them fully. So he offered, "I've told you how I've been feeling lately. I'm willing to hear anything you'd like to say to me. If you'd like to talk now, that would be fine, or if you'd like to take some time to pull your thoughts together, I'd certainly be willing to take the subject up at another time."

While Daniel did not particularly want to hear his parents' self-serving explanations, he was operating with a higher principle in mind. If he was to be heard, he would illustrate his sense of fair play by also hearing. By demonstrating good listening skills he was hoping to defuse the potential of a deepening adversarial feeling that could come between him and his parents. By no means would he drop the firmness of his convictions. In fact, he was *increasing* the likelihood that his message would be received as he chose not to get into a war of rebuttals.

Think ahead to your possible confrontation. What potential protests might the other person register against you? (For instance, "My adult son may tell me I've always tried to run his life," or "My former friend may say that everyone knows I have an uncooperative spirit.")

_____

_____

_____

What feelings will you need to guard against in the event your confrontation is rebutted? (For instance, "I've been sitting on lots of anger, and I'd need to make sure I don't become openly bitter or sarcastic," or "In my insecurity I might back down from my convictions.")

_____

_____

_____

If you decided not to defend but to listen while standing firm, what behavior would be required of you? (For instance, "I'd need to remain calm and offer no excuses for the way I feel," or "I'd need to refrain from repeating myself as I'm prone to do.")

_____

_____

_____

To help you stand firm even as you also hear the other person's protest, consider the following guidelines for such circumstances:

- Refuse to plead your case. Speaking confidently is your goal, persuasion is not.

- Don't be shocked by disagreements. Stay away from statements like, "What is the matter with you?" or "I can't *imagine* why you are so incapable of understanding the truth."

- Use a modest tone of voice, no coercion. You want your legitimate thoughts to be heard over your emotions, which might produce increased agitation.

- Explain the reasons for feeling as you do, but don't overdo it.

- Even if you sense the other person is trying to pick apart your reasoning, give minimal defense. The more you defend, the more powerful the other person feels over you.

- Don't invalidate the other person's perspective. Listen carefully, yet don't compromise your principles.

- If you sense the discussion is getting out of hand, give yourself permission to take a break from it.

Living with the Consequences

Ideally, the consequences of your confrontation would be positive. The best-case scenario would have your sense of dignity restored and a renewed respect between you and your former antagonist. We have each seen cases where this happened, and the results can be highly rewarding.

There is also the possibility, though, that the consequences of your confrontation could be less satisfactory. Are you prepared to live with that?

Daniel succeeded in staying out of an extended debate with his parents. He had said what needed to be said, now he would let time tell if they respected his position. As the months passed, his parents did, indeed, cease discussing negative matters with Brian, which pleased Daniel. This improvement did not come without a price, however. At family gatherings his parents were friendly but very superficial. As had been the case historically, they went out of their way *not* to discuss anything personal with him. Actually, this was not unusual, but because of the confrontation the superficiality seemed all the more deliberate.

Daniel decided not to make an issue of the thaw in his relationship with his parents. "Speaking in personal tones was already very uncomfortable for them," he told Dr. Minirth. "If I belabored the issue they would avoid me completely, and I'm not willing to push it to that point because it would hurt the entire extended family." The doctor nodded in agreement.

In a best-case scenario, what good consequences might come with your confrontation? (For instance, "I'd get my best friend back," or "I would now be treated with the respect I deserve.")

In a worst-case scenario, what negative consequences might come with your confrontation? (For instance, "I'd be completely misunderstood and labeled as a malcontent," or "It would spark lots of gossip about me behind my back.")

You've probably heard the saying: "Hope for the best, but prepare for the worst." Keep that in mind before you proceed.

We have discovered that some people simply cannot move forward in forgiveness without airing their legitimate needs and feelings. As these individuals proceed, we carefully remind them that life may never be quite the same after doing so. The individuals who confront will do so as they admit that *not* confronting will bring worse consequences than being open and direct.

Moving forward at this point will happen as you consider yourself free from the clutches of those who would hold you in nonproductive patterns. Are you aware of the ways you become entangled in thought patterns of control? We will explore that matter in the next chapter.

9

Releasing the Controls

Step 9. Find emotional freedom as you let go of the illusion of control.

Think of the circumstances in which you feel most emotionally secure. For instance, your security is likely to be most solid when you are in the presence of someone who accepts you as you are. Or your security is most prominent as you have just completed an accomplishment that ended exactly as you had planned. Often your security is the result of a day free from hassles or mistakes. Chances are it is enhanced when you speak clearly and you know others have taken you seriously.

Now shift gears. Think of the circumstances that produce the most emotional volatility. Volatility is likely to occur as people refuse to accept you as you are. Likewise, your volatility is enhanced as you complete a project that turned out much more poorly than antici- pated. Your emotions are less stable when your day is full of hassles and mistakes. It is worsened when your speech does not come out

163

as clearly as you would like and, as a result, others do not take you seriously.

What is a key difference between your moments of emotional stability and emotional volatility? *Control.* Your best moments are most likely to occur when you feel some amount of control in your world, when things seem tied down and in place. Conversely, your emotions are most easily unsettled when you feel a lack of control. Nothing seems to go on proper cues. You are left guessing about what problem might visit you next.

When people struggle to forgive there is invariably an accompanying feeling that life has gotten out of control. Their emotions are disrupted by rejection or deceit or manipulation or backstabbing—events outside their preferences, events that leave them feeling vulnerable to the control of others.

Mark sat across from Dr. Carter shaking his head. "Something's very unfair about my life. I give everything I've got to others, but I have very little to show for it." He had good reason to feel as he did. All his life Mark had been a reliable person, ready to help anyone else in time of need. In fact, if forced to summarize his personality in one word, it would be *conscientious.* Mark was always tuned in to the big picture and his decisions reflected a thoughtful, helpful outlook.

In his late forties, Mark was in his second marriage, and while it had its share of distractions, he was reasonably happy with his wife, Mary Dana. They had a teenage son and he, too, was a bright spot, a good kid who got along well with virtually everyone. "My problem," he explained, "is that I've got two grown daughters who won't give me a chance. My older daughter is twenty-six and married, but she never calls or visits unless she wants money. My next daughter is twenty-three going on fifteen. She's still in college because she's changed majors so many times. She keeps falling farther and farther behind. I have very little influence in her life because she's a clone of my ex-wife. They look alike and think alike, which means they're both seductive and manipulative. Brianna can be the sweetest daughter one moment, but she can turn on you in a flash. Just like her mother, she's got an awful temper, and it takes very little to provoke it."

Mark's emotional struggles reached a peak two years prior to meeting Dr. Carter when he attended the wedding of his elder daughter, Laurie. To say he felt like a fish out of water at the event would be a gross understatement. His ex-wife, Ellie, was in total control, and she had no shame in relegating Mark to the status of an outsider. At the rehearsal dinner he and Mary Dana were excluded from sitting with any family, and during the ceremony and reception they also were treated as an afterthought.

"I didn't mind so much that Ellie was rude to me," he told Dr. Carter, "because that's the way she's always been, and I don't expect anything different. But it was Laurie's behavior that really got to me. Here I was footing the bill for most of the event, and she just brushed me off royally. Her mother is a *very* dominant personality, and I'm sure Laurie didn't want to do anything to upset her. I've always stayed out of the middle with her and her mom, and until the wedding I thought we had a pretty good relationship. At least, I didn't have any major complaints.

"And you know, I could understand Laurie's awkwardness at the wedding," Mark continued, "because I know it's not easy feeling caught between your divorced parents. I guess I could get over the hurdle more easily if she had tried to make up for it in the weeks and months afterward. But in the last two years Laurie has kept her distance from me. She only lives forty minutes away, so it's not that hard for us to get together. But we've finally quit calling her to do things because she never has time. It's funny, though, she'll drop everything in order to spend time with her mother. I feel pushed aside by her, and it really hurts. It hurts deeply."

Adding insult to injury, Brianna would receive virtually no input from her dad either. "About a year ago I learned that she'd let her boyfriend move into her apartment with her. When I found out about it I told her I couldn't continue paying her bills if she was going to shack up with some guy I didn't even know. She said she understood, but our relationship has never been the same."

"Have you discussed these things with your daughters?"

"Oh yes. Last summer I had both of them at my house for a day, and we had a long talk. I told them how much I loved them and I didn't want our differences to come between us. But the deeper we went in our conversation, the worse it got. Just like their mother, they both became very defensive and wouldn't hear a word I said. Since then, we've just had superficial contact, and unless something dramatic happens, I don't see any improvement for a long time."

Then with a look of resolve Mark said, "I just wish I could *make* those young women straighten up and fly right. There's so much good that could come if they did as I tell them to do."

What was Mark's problem? Definitely he needed to forgive his daughters for their lack of respect and for their disloyalty to his good intentions. He was having difficulty doing so, though, because events with them were not following his script. He was yearning for a position of control in their lives that would not be. The result was his unforgiving spirit.

Have you had out-of-control feelings that added to your difficulty in forgiving? Has the other person seemed intent on doing things in direct disregard of your belief structure? If so, you, like Mark, may find forgiveness difficult until you decide how you will handle this dimension.

In what circumstances have you felt controlled by someone who is in the wrong? (For instance, "My parents dangle money in front of me to entice me to do things their way," or "No amount of pleading can force my brother-in-law to cooperate with family plans.")

_____

_____

_____

How does this element of control affect your emotions? (For instance, "When my parents try to control me I withdraw in disgust," or "When my brother-in-law is stubborn I argue with him."

———————————————————————————————
———————————————————————————————
———————————————————————————————

Let's examine two different angles to the problem of control. First, let's recognize how problems are created by others' controlling ways; then let's look at how you might add to those problems by responding with countercontrol tactics.

To determine your susceptibility to being controlled, check the following statements that apply to you:

__ There are people in my world who emphasize performance over relationships.

__ I often feel that my life is driven by obligations.

__ With certain people in my life, mistakes are met with scorn or judgment.

__ People in my world will tell me what they think I should do, even when I haven't asked their advice.

__ Others seem to think that I shouldn't act or think too differently from the way they do.

__ I get the sense that I'm supposed to fit the mold others have defined for me.

__ With certain people, I tend to hold back my thoughts and feelings because I don't want to deal with the frustration that would come with being open.

__ Too much of my time is spent dodging someone else's irritable mood.

__ I have been on the receiving end of others' manipulations.

__ I get the sense I'm not supposed to have the perspectives or feelings that I have.

__ When working on a project around key people, I feel as if someone is looking over my shoulder.

__ When I attempt to explain my point of view it is often met by a rebuttal or an invalidation of my perspective.

We all have moments when we feel controlled, but the more frequently this happens to you, the more difficulty you will encounter in forgiving. If you checked six or more statements it indicates that you probably find yourself regularly frustrated with someone else's controlling behavior. Your task will be to remain unhooked from their mandates as you separately plan how you will pursue forgiveness on your own.

Now let's consider the potential for you to respond to someone's controlling behavior with your own controlling responses. Be honest as you examine the following statements to determine which ones apply to you:

__ When faced with someone's controlling behavior I get caught in reactions of annoyance or irritability.

__ Around controlling people I won't discuss my emotions or perspectives.

__ There are times when my opinions are very strong, to the extent that I could be described as stubborn.

__ I can struggle with critical thoughts.

__ When around controlling people I act more defensively than I would like.

__ I don't like my decisions or beliefs to be second-guessed.

__ I become impatient with others' lack of cooperation.

__ In my private moments I dream about how my life should be better.

__ After an encounter with a controlling person I second-guess the way I should have handled it.

__ I get caught in arguments when I really should know better.

__ I'll admit that I can expend too much energy protesting another person's foul treatment.

___ When expressing my opinions my tone of voice can become persuasive.

Every person has moments of desiring control, so it would be unusual if you could not check any of the items. If you checked six or more there is a strong possibility that you will respond to others' control with your own brand of countercontrol. In doing so, you are susceptible to an unforgiving spirit.

As Dr. Carter discussed family problems with Mark, he explained that the desire for control or predictability was normal, yet he would need to be careful not to go overboard in pushing his beliefs on others. "I can certainly appreciate how you'd like your daughters to be grateful for the many sacrifices you've made for them. You have solid motives as a dad and it'd be nice if they could recognize that."

"You know, I'm not asking for anything out of the ordinary," Mark explained. "I know that their mother is going to be a more dominant force in their lives because that's always been her personality. I'd just like to get Brianna and Laurie to understand that they owe their father some respect."

Think about the moments when you protest the controlling circumstances in your life. What is *legitimate* about your desires? (For instance, "It's legitimate that I'd want my parents to be encouragers rather than critics," or "It's legitimate that I don't care for my former friend's gossiping ways.")

_____

_____

_____

Now be honest about your management of those legitimate thoughts. How can your reasonable convictions cross the line, leading you toward unhealthy, controlling behaviors? (For instance, "When I try to get my sister to listen to my common sense,

I become too overpowering in my speech," or "A spirit of judgment comes over me as I see my son defying my rules.")

_____

_____

_____

Acknowledging Others' Freedom

Structure, accountability, and correctness: These characteristics are part of a life anchored in responsibility. It is good to place a premium on traits such as these. But here is the catch. (You knew there would be one, didn't you?) From mankind's beginning, God has put free will into the equation as we determine how we will or will not live. In order for any decision to have meaning or purpose, it must be accompanied by the option of doing its opposite. This means risk since there is always the potential that someone else will view their options differently from yours. Freedom creates the potential for great conflict, to the extent that we are often tempted to deny another's privilege of choice.

Dr. Carter addressed this issue with Mark. "In a sense, your difficulty in forgiving your daughters is hindered by your common sense." A puzzled look crossed Mark's face as the doctor explained. "You're so convinced of the appropriateness of your beliefs that it's nearly impossible to let your girls live otherwise."

"You need to understand," Mark replied, "that I *love* my daughters. Next to my wife, my children are the most precious things that I have. It eats me alive to know that the girls' mother has wielded such an influence that they can't extend common courtesies, much less appreciation, to me."

"It would be easier for you to proceed with forgiveness if I could somehow convince you that your convictions were wrong," said Dr. Carter, "but I happen to agree with your assessment. It really would be best if they could show loyalty and love toward you." He paused before making his point. "You're never going to forgive if you cling to the wish that you could make them believe correctly as you do. I'm not suggesting for a moment that you should drop your convictions. That would be irresponsible. But I *am* suggesting that you not be stuck in an emotional dungeon that results from falsely thinking that somehow you might be able to control their decisions. Forgiveness begins as you recognize their freedom to be who they are, even if they choose wrong paths."

Acknowledging freedom can feel very uncomfortable. If you are struggling to forgive it is probably because someone freely chose to hurt you or manipulate you or slander you. Naturally you wish to control such choices because you want to prevent the potential of a repeat performance. Hard truth, though, says you can't control another's choices.

As you survey the choices of the person who hurt you, what error in thinking was that person using? (For instance, "My husband rationalized it was okay to bring pornography into our home," or "My boss feels it is her right to act as underhandedly as she wants.")

_____

_____

_____

Now here is the hard question. Can you recognize that person's freedom to live as he or she chooses, even if it is dead wrong? The thought can be unsettling.

Mark contemplated the doctor's words for a moment, then said, "So I'm just supposed to let go and allow my daughters to live with a haughty, unappreciative attitude toward their father. Is that what you're suggesting that I do?"

"I'm not suggesting that the option you just stated is a pleasant or desirable one. I am simply suggesting that you line your thoughts up with reality, even if it is unpleasant." Then Dr. Carter explained, "I'm operating with two beliefs in mind. The first is, control is an illusion. The second is, freedom is reality." He paused to let Mark soak in the words.

"I've never heard it put quite like that before. This one's going to take some real thought."

Whether we like the results or not, it is a reality that people are free to be whatever they choose. No wishing or coercion or intimidation can change the fact that people can choose their own directions.

What makes it difficult for you to accept the stark reality of freedom? (For instance, "How can I endorse my wife's freedom when she chooses to be so passive and lazy?" or "I hate that my father freely chooses to deny the fact that he has a drinking problem.")

_____

_____

_____

Moving Forward in Your Own Freedom

In order to prevent you from being too disillusioned by freedom, let's turn the focus away from the wrongdoer and onto yourself. Just as others are free to choose their own directions in life, you, too, can proceed with the privilege of choices. In Chapter 3, for instance, we discussed how you can manage your bitterness by first acknowledging your freedom to hold on to it. Ultimately, this can cause you to question why you would choose not to be bitter. The net result can be that you would become more fully responsible as you freely sift out the pros and cons of each option before you.

Let's apply this concept to the matter of control. If you choose, you can continue to speak coercively to the ones you are in conflict with. You can plead your case loudly. You can quietly withdraw as a form of manipulation. You can use heavy-handed tactics to get your way. These are free possibilities.

Be honest. What nonproductive choices have you contemplated as you have interacted with the wrongdoers in your life? (For in-

stance, "I've tried to force my brother to go along with my preferences regarding holiday plans," or "I've chosen to control by
withholding affection.")

_____

_____

_____

By recognizing your freedom to utilize maladaptive behaviors you
may become more willing to consider the better alternatives. For
instance, with the doctor's help Mark realized he could speak coercively or dogmatically to his daughters in order to get their respect.
He realized, however, that he would get poor returns on this style of
communication. He concluded that even though he might not get the
desired result from his daughters, he could also freely choose to
accept them as they are, deficits and all.

"That's not easy or natural," he admitted. "I'd rather force my way
into their minds and make them think as I want, but I'm realizing
I'd be setting myself up to be held captive by their every move."

Mark was making good insights. He was admitting to himself his
limitations regarding his ability to force certain attitudes or behaviors in his girls. Rather than remaining stuck in the painful emotions
accompanying the control fantasy, he was realizing that he could
still use freedom to choose his own emotional direction even if his
daughters remained in their unloving state.

How can the awareness of your own freedom guide you toward
the most responsible reactions to another's wrong deeds? (For
instance, "I'm free to say no to my brother's unrealistic requests,
even if he has other plans for me," or "I can allow myself to pick
and choose which family gatherings I will attend, based on what
seems best to me.")

_____

_____

_____

Keys to Overcoming Control

Disengaging from the control game is accomplished as you develop key attitudes and beliefs, which then influence your behavior and emotional choices. Let's examine four keys we have found helpful in the process of avoiding control problems.

Key 1. Make Room for Lousy Circumstances

If you remain caught in a controlling style of thinking, it is probable that you are clinging to unrealistic ideals. We are not suggesting that your ideals are bad, mind you, just unrealistic. For instance, Mark regularly asked his wife, Mary Dana, "What's the deal with the generation behind us? Why don't they have respect for their elders anymore?" He could wax eloquent about how Brianna and Laurie should appreciate all the things he had done for them. Couldn't they see how he bent over backward to accommodate conflicting family schedules? Didn't they appreciate how he had helped them financially on many occasions? Didn't they understand how fortunate they were that, unlike some men, he *liked* to communicate about personal issues?

Mark frequently used words like *should* or *ought to* or *had better* as he talked about how his daughters were supposed to respond to him. This fed his tendency to control since his "shoulds" were so correct. But there was one major truth he was ignoring in his idealistic thinking. His daughters didn't care what he thought "should" be. Every time he encountered their contrary attitudes and held staunchly to his ideals, he was less able to accept and forgive them. Strangely, his ideals were sabotaging his emotional stability.

In what circumstances have you held to ideals only to realize that the other person didn't care about your priorities or beliefs? (For instance, "I've tried to insist to my husband that he should take greater interest in our kids' spiritual development, but he won't," or "I think my uncle should openly apologize for his bad behavior, but that will never happen.")

_____

_____

_____

As you hold to your ideals, how is your ability to forgive hindered? (For instance, "I can't let go of my anger toward my husband until I convince him to be a better leader toward our children," or "Critical thoughts fester in my mind as my uncle continues in his same old insensitivities.")

_____

_____

_____

Dr. Carter spoke with Mark about the negative impact of holding so tightly to his ideals. "In a strange way you're being hindered by your sense of correctness. You're so right in your thoughts that you've convinced yourself that you must make your girls see things your way. But the more you wish to control them, the more out of control your emotions become."

"So are you suggesting that I let go of my correctness?"

"Not at all. I _am_ suggesting, though, that you recognize your daughters' right to be wrong. Make room for the potential that they will be mistake makers. Remember that control is an illusion. Your wish to control them will only keep you _more_ imprisoned by your own painful emotions."

It's hard to make room for lousy circumstances when your control thoughts inhibit you from accepting another person's freedoms. What adjustments will you need to make as you accept the reality that others will freely choose wrong paths? (For instance, "I'll need to make room for the fact that my mother-in-law will never accept me. I'll quit expressing shock over her harsh attitudes," or "I'll recognize that my brother lives with chronic denial of his problems, and it's not my job to make him see the light.")

_____

_____

_____

Key 2. Remember That Some People Are Afraid of Growth

If you are searching for ways to improve your emotional balance, it is because you are committed to personal growth and improvement. You should be commended for this! As you are in your growth mode, it is only natural that you would want others to join you. It is at this point that you may encounter trouble. Some people don't want to change, no matter how right the adjustments are. "No thanks," they'll state, "I'm perfectly satisfied to keep on living as I always have."

Have you ever experienced that type of stubbornness? If you are struggling to forgive, there is a high probability that it is caused by the wrongdoer's unwillingness to change.

What is your natural response to that stubbornness? You want to rub it out. You want to take control and erase the traits that are harming forward movement.

Trying to make a resistant person change is like trying to pull a mule who won't go forward. The mule will win! Your effort to control will leave you feeling controlled, and as long as you engage in a power play or a war of the wills your emotions will deteriorate.

What emotions have you experienced as you've realized you can't control the person who refuses to change? (For instance, "My rage reaches a boiling point because my husband won't admit he's so insensitive," or "I've come to hate my former employer because he's so unreasonable with every person he's managed.")

_____

_____

_____

Recognize that ultimately you lose as you yearn for control over someone who won't succumb to your control. You will need to alter your thoughts and behaviors in order to disentangle from the emotional web that keeps you from forgiving.

Mark told Dr. Carter, "Common sense tells me you're right when you say I can't control my daughters, but I want so badly for things to be better that it's hard for me just to lie down and say nothing. I feel as though I'm being disloyal to my own beliefs if I let go."

"Right now I want you to focus less on forcing things to happen so you can focus more on creating a healthy pattern of emotional management. Over the long run your daughters will return to you only if they see consistency in your emotions. By forgiving them and accepting them as they are, your influence will increase. The great unknown in the equation, though, is whether they want to be influenced at all."

Be willing to look behind the scenes of the other person's refusal to change; usually you will discover fear. Mark's daughters were afraid of offending their mother who was more judgmental than Mark. They wanted to love him, but they knew it would come at a high cost. Once Brianna told him, "Dad, if I show favoritism to you, Mom will go ballistic, and I'm not sure I could deal with it."

Change is very threatening to some people for varying reasons. Change might mean:

- Having to admit weaknesses or expose insecurities.

- Dealing with the rejection of those who are not committed to healthy priorities.

177

- Entering a way of life that is very different and new.

- Becoming open and vulnerable, meaning there is an unknown element to the future.

- Admitting lies or admitting poor choices.

- Having to say "I was wrong" or "I'm sorry."

Think about the persons in your life who refuse to change. What fear drives them? (For instance, "Behind my father's gruff exterior is the fear of being dominated," or "My wife is afraid to love because of emotional pain in her past.")

_____

_____

_____

Knowing that fear may be behind the resistant person's stubbornness does not necessarily make your task easier, but it can create objectivity, a trait necessary for you to move forward with your rational choices in response to difficult circumstances. As you realize how fear drives others' poor choices, you can then see that their rejection of you is really a reflection of their imperfections, not yours. This awareness can help you to disengage from power games.

Key 3. Realize that Some People Will Be Permanently Unaware

Dr. Carter spoke candidly with Mark. "I'm not ready yet to give up on your daughters. They're still young enough to learn new lessons and correct some of their patterns of dealing with you. Your ex-wife, however, is much farther down the road than your daugh ters, and it sounds as if she has shown no inclination to change. Her strong influence on Brianna and Laurie may not bode well for you."

"I've thought the same thing myself. In the past, I've talked hours with my ex in an attempt to get her to loosen up on her all-or-nothing thinking. She's just like her mother was, rigid and very judgmental. Once you get on her bad list, like the one I'm on, no pleading in the world will make her see things differently. Her mind is set in cement."

Would the daughters be the next in succession with this same attitude? We could not say for sure. Dr. Carter did suggest, "You may need to leave room for the possibility that some people seem to possess virtually no capacity for insight. You'll need to make your emotional choices separate from their habits or tendencies."

One of the most interesting phenomena we have experienced through the years is the fact that individuals can vary so widely in the ability to incorporate insight. Some just need a nudge from the doctor and they are well on their way toward tremendous awareness and changes. In other cases, we can speak eloquently about helpful insights with no positive results. Why is this? The answer is impossible to find. There are too many conflicting explanations to say why some people simply cannot or will not change. Suffice to say, though, that there is a wide difference in the levels of awareness that people have regarding their emotional and relational choices.

Though you certainly may not know why another person may never change, are you willing to admit that some people may never develop the insight and awareness that are so necessary for change?

What evidence might indicate that your wrongdoer is so unaware that change may never happen? (For instance, "Several respected people have talked with my brother about his inappropriate attitude toward women, yet he continues his rudeness as he always has," or "My mother has heard hundreds of sermons about love and kindness, yet she persists in rationalizing her critical, rejecting spirit.")

_____

_____

_____

Even Christ Himself encountered people who would not change (for instance, the rich young ruler who is described in Matt. 19:16–26). He loved anyone who came His way, yet He also chose not to push Himself on people who would not incorporate His thoughts. By letting go of any need to control such people He was able to maintain control over His life's direction.

You, too, may need to concede that some people are "unaware" and will not respond to your words of wisdom. As you do, your behavior can be affected in several ways:

- You can use a noncoercive style of speech, knowing that pleading and persuading will only keep you ensnared in anger or disillusionment.

- In discussions with the offending person you will stop repeating yourself as you realize the next time you give the same speech you'll get the same frustrating results.

- You can commit your time and efforts to relationships that will be more satisfying.

- You can have permission not to spend as much time with the obstinate person.

- Your emotional stability will be determined by your own choices, not the other person's compliance.

While it may not be pleasant to admit how unaware some people can be, your willingness to accept this reality can represent a major breakthrough in your ability to forgive. How can the acknowledgment of another person's "unawareness" help you forgive? (For instance, "If I stop arguing with my mother I'll feel much more calm," or "Realizing my ex-wife will always be unable to see my improvements, I can move forward without getting caught in angry protests about her.")

Key 4. Realize the Paradox of Letting Go of Control

At this point, let's reinforce a major thought: We *do* stand for structure, principles, godly absolutes, and firmness. Sometimes as we discuss the concept of letting go of control and accepting freedom's reality, we hear the protest: "But I don't want to have to lie down and let the other person have his way with me. I'll not be trampled on!"

We operate under the assumption that the best way to be in control is to quit trying so desperately to be in control. Or to put the principle in other terms, the best way to go out of control is to try to control everything!

Most people strongly resist being controlled because of the innate desire we each have to be in control. Simply put, people do not like being put into slots. They do not want to be told how to feel or what improvements should be made or how to respond to others' needs.

Mark reflected quite a bit about his diminishing influence over his girls. In one session he admitted to Dr. Carter, "When they were teenagers both Brianna and Laurie complained that I gave more advice than they wanted to hear, and maybe they were right. Maybe I've got too many notions about the way they should act, and they've grown tired of hearing it."

Dr. Carter recalled, "A man once told me, 'I'm so right that I'm wrong.' When he said that, the clarity of his words really struck a chord with me. This man realized that his correct knowledge gave him 'permission' to be critical and bossy and intrusive. I realized he was speaking for many of us, myself included, by saying he was so right he was wrong."

When you speak messages of persuasion and control, accompanying your spoken words are covert messages that sabotage the truthfulness of your words. When you are hardheaded or too dogmatic or highly insistent, without ever saying it, the person receiving your words covertly hears:

- "I don't accept you at all."

- "I don't trust you."

- "Why don't you let me do your thinking for you?"

- "I'm superior to you."

- "It's your job to live inside my box."

Though your spoken words may make all the sense in the world, a controlling attitude sends covert messages that completely undermine your influence.

By letting go of a controlling attitude, you portray a calm, perhaps even accepting, spirit that is void of such covert messages. Then and only then, will you have any lasting influence over others, if you will have any influence at all. Even if you do not succeed in positively affecting the other person, you can succeed in keeping your own reactions under control.

To gain better control of your own emotional direction, what controlling thoughts will you set aside? (For instance, "I'll stop insisting that my sister-in-law should think nice thoughts about me," or "I'll stop obsessing about how I could get my dad to accept my husband.")

_____

_____

_____

Setting aside control means you admit just how limited you are. By letting go of the illusion of control, what limits are you admitting to? (For instance, "I'm limited in forcing my former friends to see that I've truly grown from my past mistakes," or "I'm limited in making my spouse have the same parenting goals as I do; I can't run interference.")

_____

_____

_____

Your challenge is to choose forgiveness even if people and circumstances are outside your control. Are you up to it? Your own free determination to forgive will happen only as you incorporate forgiveness in your overall priorities for life. We will explore this concept in the next chapter.

10

Defining Your Mission

Step 10. Choose forgiveness because it is part of your life's mission.

When you realize how wrong a person has acted toward you, feelings of hurt and betrayal and grief and dismay will dominate. As these feelings become prominent, you are likely to remind yourself, perhaps at someone else's prompting, that you are supposed to forgive. Your conscience wrestles with the thought: *Good people are supposed to forgive. I can't let myself give in to my anger and hurt.* This notion is, of course, a good one, yet it can create problems if it is propelled largely by duty.

Remember Marcia? She was the mid-thirties single woman who had mixed feelings whenever she would visit her parents. Her mother was nurturing and sweet, but her father was gruff and condescending and easily angered. Marcia and Dr. Carter had discussed at length how it was not necessary to succumb to the position of inferiority each time her father tried acting superior toward her. She had made

185

excellent adjustments in speaking to him as an equal even though he did not think of her as his equal. She had rethought the foundations for her self-esteem and had rightly concluded that God would be the ultimate source of her well-being. Though Dad wanted to be in the god-position, she was learning to successfully avoid the trap of letting him dictate her sense of self-worth.

"I've got to admit," Marcia told the doctor, "that I'm a lot better than I used to be when I have to visit home. Dad is no longer the intimidator to me that he once was. I can hold my own now, thanks to some new insights and better choices in handling my emotions."

Shaking her head slowly she admitted, "The whole notion of forgiveness has one major hitch in it. As much as I want to be forgiving, I don't really see Dad showing any realization that he's done anything wrong. How can I forgive someone who won't even admit *any* guilt?"

Marcia had not only made good personal adjustments, she had carefully discussed with her father her concerns about memories of her verbal and physical abuse. She had written her feelings down and had asked him to hear her fully, which he did. His only response to her confrontation, however, was, "Seems to me that you and I remember things entirely different. Maybe if you were a parent you'd realize that things aren't as easy as it might seem, trying to keep young'uns in line."

She protested when he spoke, but when he went stubbornly silent she decided that no amount of confronting would change him, so she decided to drop the subject for good. "How can I forgive such an old goat?" she asked Dr. Carter. "My only motivation to forgive is the fact that the Bible says we're supposed to do it. But I'll tell you, it's not natural."

Have you ever had similar feelings? What circumstance has been difficult for you in the sense that forgiveness seemed too good for the other person? (For instance, "My father was terribly abusive,

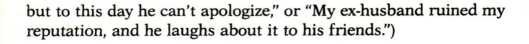

but to this day he can't apologize," or "My ex-husband ruined my reputation, and he laughs about it to his friends.")

When you are in the midst of that struggle, what lectures about forgiveness does your conscience give you? (For instance, "Christ forgave His killers, so I should be like Him," or "I wonder if I've really resolved my problems since I still hold hate.")

Don't assume that your struggle makes you abnormal. Rarely is forgiveness the easiest or most natural path to take, particularly when the offending person is unrepentant. Since earliest childhood you learned that wrongs are supposed to be confronted and eliminated. The wrongs committed against you were unfair, so naturally you want to see fairness win, just as you had been taught. What are you to do, though, when unfairness reigns?

That was Marcia's dilemma. "You know, this whole problem would be made easier if I could just sense that Daddy was willing to make some restitution," she explained to the doctor. "I remember several years ago when I was jilted by a boyfriend. We had dated for two years and had discussed marriage, but he got cold feet and just deserted me. I was really hurt and angry, but in time we were able to talk it out. He admitted his wrong and shared with me on a very deep level how he felt unsure about his ability to be a good husband. I was still hurt, but I was able to move on to forgive him because we at least had the chance to be honest with each other."

Summarizing, Dr. Carter replied, "So you'd like to see your father talk with the same level of honesty and vulnerability. The past pain wouldn't be erased, yet you would feel free to move on."

"That's exactly what I'm getting at." Then, rolling her eyes, Marcia said, "But it will never happen. It's just not fair that he should get off without at least admitting his wrongs."

Have you had similar thoughts? What is most unfair about your circumstances, making forgiveness difficult? (For instance, "Since I parted ways with my best friend, she's been lying about what caused our relationship to break up, but I can't prove it," or "My son has been very manipulative, yet he won't admit how disruptive he's been to our entire family.")

_____

_____

_____

Dr. Carter discussed a concept with Marcia that is crucial to those seeking to forgive in the midst of unwanted circumstances. "There is a great deal at stake here as you determine what to do with your feelings about your father. Ultimately you are trying to decide if you can pursue your own independent plan for emotional stability even in the midst of no cooperation. You are basically asking yourself, 'Can I do what I know is right and best even as I realize he is doing what is wrong and not the best?'" She nodded her head as she contemplated the implications of what was being discussed.

The doctor continued. "If you are ever going to stay on a steady emotional path, it will be accomplished only as you decide what traits will be dominant in your personality even if you get no outside help to make those traits a reality. You need to see yourself on a mission that is mapped out by you and the Lord."

Do you have your own independent mission statement guiding your life? Most organizations will chart their course based on their statement of purpose. For instance, a civic organization may have specific plans to establish and maintain certain services within the community. A church may feel specially appointed to reach people with their beliefs about God's plan for salvation. A branch of government will spell out its function as it defines what services it will provide.

What about you? Though you are just one person, you, too, can operate with your own distinct sense of purpose. What is your mission in life?

Such a question cannot be answered lightly. It requires deep introspection before God. Dr. Carter closed a session with Marcia by asking her to write out a statement of purpose for her life, to define her mission. The next time she saw him she admitted, "That was probably one of the most challenging assignments I've undertaken. I had to set aside what everyone else might have written for me so I could write exactly what I believe."

Here is what she wrote: "My mission in life is to know God's love in such a way that it would directly affect the way I relate with others. I am to be a conduit of godly love to those I encounter, being always willing to display the fruit of the Spirit both in behavior and in attitude."

How about you? Take some time to ponder your mission in life. What are you trying to accomplish? What will define you? Write here a statement that would summarize that mission.

_____

_____

_____

_____

It's not easy, is it? It's one thing to nod in agreement when you hear someone else talk about the virtues of being kind or loving or giving. It's an entirely different matter, though, to claim ownership of such concepts. To do so you have to have deep belief and commitment.

Notice two major elements that are probably *not* in your mission statement. If you are like most people you did not include: (1) the wish to be angry, insecure, or resentful, or (2) the requirement that key people have to first act rightly so you can get on with your mission.

Marcia chuckled as Dr. Carter pointed these two things out to her. "All right, you've made your point. I'm supposed to be what I want to be because of my commitment to my mission, not because my dad finally started acting right."

That said, the doctor quietly nodded in agreement. She'd hit the nail on the head.

We believe that a truly successful mission includes a forgiving spirit, not necessarily because the persons receiving the forgiveness deserve it, but because it is consistent with the character of our ultimate role model, Jesus Christ. Only by forgiving can you be free to pursue such qualities as love and security and servitude. Forgiveness cleanses you of the traits that will tie you to a life of misery and discord.

Be Aware of Dependencies

As you take initiatives to live out your mission, there is a personality trait you will need to keep in close check. That trait is dependency, the tendency to let your emotions and attitudes and behaviors be determined by outside people and circumstances.

Before you quickly decide that you are not a dependent person, realize that every one of us has this quality within. It is dependency that causes you to want affirmation, to respond with impatience when someone is slow, to be cautious when speaking to a controlling person, to feel grateful when someone is helpful, to feel hurt when a loved one lets you down. Because you are linked through your emotional responses to other people, you can be labeled as dependent.

As you establish forgiveness as part of your life's overall initiative, you will not need to eliminate your dependency. That is neither possible or desirable. Rather, you will need to keep your dependencies balanced so you are not too easily pulled off course by someone else's lack of cooperation.

Try to identify some moments when your mission was too powerfully dependent upon others' actions. Through the years we have noticed some common circumstances that keep people from being who they would like to be. Can you identify with any of them?

- Your spouse has lied to you, but you cannot prove him or her wrong, the result being tremendous anger because the relationship cannot move forward in honesty.

- A family member stubbornly continues to act in ways that undermine your principles of fair play.

- No matter how clearly you confront a person about a problem, that problem persists.

- A close friend has betrayed your trust, leaving you feeling wounded and alone.

- A person you hoped would be an encourager turns out to be a critic.

- You consider yourself to be loyal and reliable, but certain key people do not maintain loyalty toward you.

- A friend or family member simply quits on the relationship with you.

Many such circumstances will evoke painful feelings from you, which is normal. What is worse, though, these circumstances can also drain you of your motivation to stay within your mission. Your motivation may hinge so heavily on outside forces that you can lose your will to live rightly.

In what situation have you lost your sense of mission because of someone else's undesirable behavior? (For instance, "When my wife divorced me I started drinking heavily and living selfishly," or "Since my friend backstabbed me I've lost my confidence, and I won't let anyone get to know me.")

_____

_____

_____

By handing your motivation over to people and circumstances, your dependency goes out-of-bounds. This implies you have given up on your skills and initiatives, leaving you vulnerable to inner traits that you would not normally choose to dominate your personality.

How is it that your mission can be lost to circumstances? We have found that most people do not consciously or deliberately turn over their mission to outside forces. Rather, it is a habit that stems from patterns usually learned in the early years of development. To get an idea of whether your sense of mission is lost because of poorly developed habits, see how many of the following statements apply to you:

— During my early years I didn't talk deeply with my parents about emotional struggles.
— I was told how I should live but not given room to ask questions that would help me understand why.
— As a teen, I was more interested in making the right grade than in actually learning concepts and truths.
— In my past, I was reluctant to fully reveal my insecurities and uncertainties.
— While I may not always have complied with every rule, I learned that compliance wins the favor of those in authority over me.
— Too often I kept my curiosities to myself.
— Guilt was used in motivating me to do what was correct.

___ I didn't read many books other than the ones assigned to me as part of school projects.

___ I learned that the way to stay out of trouble was to keep my mouth shut whenever I disagreed with authorities.

___ When I felt angry, I was told how to behave but not how to explore why I felt as I did.

Most children had an emphasis on compliance when they were growing up, so if you checked some of the items, that is normal. If you checked six or more, though, it is likely that you were not openly or consistently encouraged to take ownership of the direction of your motivating thoughts. You may have been told what to do or how you should think, but that is not the same as being encouraged to think deeply about the meaning and direction of your emotions.

A large percentage of people do not really exert the necessary effort needed to define their mission in life until forced to do so by a crisis. If that is the case with you, don't think of yourself as odd. Be glad that you are at a point of contemplating who you will be.

Ideally, you would have been encouraged as a young person to define for yourself who you would be. If that had happened, you would be less likely to be dependent on circumstances to define you. But in the absence of such encouragement, there is still hope. Beginning today you can chart your own course, determining what your mission will be.

Marcia liked the implications of what Dr. Carter was telling her. "Never in a million years would my father talk with me about the directions I could take in my emotions. My mother was willing to talk on a personal level with me, but she didn't really understand how to get me to establish a mission." Then with a spark in her eye she added, "It's never too late to get started, so there's no time like the present. This has been long overdue, so no more delay!"

Could you take that same attitude? Perhaps, like Marcia, you were not trained in your early years to think about what your mission would be, but is there anything stopping you today? Our guess is that you *want* to be a forgiving person, and you can be as you fit it into your overall initiative regarding your purpose.

What would have to change as you determine to live according to your own well-conceived mission? (For instance, "I'd stop hoping for my dad to give me his approval before I can proceed confidently in my life," or "I'd determine to stay on my course even if it meant losing my friend's agreement.")

_____

_____

_____

On a Mission Toward Forgiveness

Your efforts to be forgiving would be made easier if the wrongdoers would become totally honest about how they have harmed you. If they could register genuine remorse that, too, would make your goal more attainable. In a few cases this will actually happen, and when it does, consider yourself fortunate. In most cases your antagonists will not be cooperative, making your task less natural.

Whether your wrongdoer asks genuinely for forgiveness or deserves it, make it your separate goal to sustain the personality traits necessary for your own emotional stability. Make forgiveness an act of initiative, not dependent on the attitudes or behaviors of others.

Before we explore some of the necessary ingredients for a mission toward forgiveness, think carefully about the traits you want to lead the way in your personality. What qualities do you want most to be known for? (For instance, "I'd like to be known as a fair-minded person, willing to give people a chance," or "I want a loving spirit to guide me.")

_____

_____

_____

Now ask, Can I sustain those qualities even if others in my world do not share similar positive goals? For instance, Marcia highly respected her mother's powerful patience. She told the doctor she would like this quality to be at the top of her list of dominant personal characteristics. He asked her, "Can you envision yourself being patient even in moments when your father is noncooperative or critical?"

You, too, can take upon yourself a similar challenge. Your mission need not be empowered and sustained by humans. Instead, you can use God's guidance to carry you. As you spell out your desired qualities, can you, like Marcia, see yourself living them out regardless of the behavior of others?

Let's explore four of the most necessary ingredients as you establish a mission toward forgiveness.

Love

Surely you are familiar with the incident when the young lawyer asked Christ to identify the greatest of all commandments. His response was firm and to the point: "'You shall love the LORD your God with all your heart, with all your soul, and with all your mind.' This is the first and great commandment. And the second is like it: 'You shall love your neighbor as yourself'" (Matt. 22:37–39). Jesus succinctly concluded that the highest goal in life is to love.

Has love become to you just another idealistic word that belongs in romantic songs and poems? Let's hope not. Far from being a fluffy, dreamers-only trait, to love fully is to know success in life. To love means you are sufficiently at peace with your Maker and with yourself that you can extend messages of peace to those in your path. It implies that your life has direction, that you choose to extend yourself to others.

Marcia thought long and hard about how love could be a core ingredient in her life's mission. "It's virtually impossible to deny the importance of love," she reflected. "After all, who would admit that they aspire to be indifferent or hateful toward others?" But then she added, "You might easily guess that I gave up loving Dad a long time ago, probably in my teen years. I mean, I love him in the sense that he's my father, I'm not *that* cold. But I don't love who he is nor do I love being in his presence. That's been squelched for a long time."

Wanting to be sensitive, Dr. Carter stated, "I know it seems unfair to suggest that you should love someone who has not really been very lovable. Common sense tells us it would be phony to ask you to conjure up warm and fuzzy feelings for him, particularly after living with the grief he's created in your life."

Continuing, he said, "Let's focus, instead, on making love a major part of your lifestyle with the many other people you encounter each week. Does that seem like a reasonable plan?"

"Absolutely. I like feeling as if I have something meaningful to offer most people."

"Okay, with that in mind can you decide not to harbor ill will toward your father because you know you don't need it cluttering your ability to live as productively as you want with others?"

"That I can do," she said. She determined that she wanted to forgive her father because she wanted to be a loving person. Realistically she admitted that her commitment to love would probably not include sweet and flowery interludes with her dad since that would never be authentic. She could, however, choose forgiveness because she did not want ill feelings toward him to hinder her from loving people in general.

Marcia took the definition of love as described in 1 Corinthians 13:4–7 and developed a behavioral game plan:

- She would exhibit patience instead of irritability when faced with his grouchy moods.

- She would behave and speak kindly, not because he deserved it but because that's the way she wanted to be.

- She would choose not to hold herself above him as if he were inferior. She felt sorry for the fact that he was unable to relate as an equal.

- She would not respond to his rude comments with rude responses.

- She chose not to force her preferences and desires upon him, even when she was clearly right and he was clearly wrong.

- She would not accept his invitations to argue or speak caustically.

- She would refrain from discussing his contrariness behind his back.

Notice that Marcia was not required to let go of her boundaries to act in a pattern consistent with love, nor did she have to fake pleasant feelings that did not exist. She decided to live in accordance with her mature choices rather than letting her behavior be dependent upon her father's immaturity.

What is it about your wrongdoer that makes love a difficult task? (For instance, "My mother-in-law is completely self-absorbed and can't relate to anyone's needs but her own," or "My sister consistently has an arrogant and hateful attitude.")

_____

_____

_____

Be glad your ability to love can be a choice drawn from within yourself rather than being dependent upon the right circumstances.

Even if you never *feel* loving toward your wrongdoer, what key traits could you exhibit to illustrate you are committed to an overall life of love? (For instance, "I'll choose to sidestep the opportunity to argue," or "I can cease giving glaring looks and act polite instead.")

_____

_____

_____

_____

Keep in mind that Christ, the consummate embodiment of love, had to contend with people who hated Him to the point of wanting Him dead. It is doubtful that He was ever able to be on good terms with many of His antagonists, yet in spite of their misguided lives, He forgave because it was in His character to do so. To not forgive would have negated the fullness of His love toward those able to receive Him.

Respect

Close on the heels of love as a necessary ingredient for a person on a mission toward forgiveness is respect. Just as it may seem that some people are not lovable, it may also seem that some are deserving of no respect. After all, you may ask, how can persons be respected when they have lied or manipulated or deserted or abused?

What is it about your wrongdoer that you disrespect? (For instance, "My ex-husband thinks women are meant to be used," or "My former friend constantly lies about me and falsely builds herself up at my expense.")

_____

_____

_____

Your feelings of hurt or disillusionment or anger are legitimate, and you should not be required to pretend that you feel otherwise. But as we discussed about love, your commitment to be respectful does not have to be dependent upon the other person's behavior. If that were the case, you might never be able to respect!

Respect is defined as treating others in the same worthy manner as you would like to be treated. It implies that you will act with dignity and tact. *Respect does not have to be earned,* as some might assume. It is a trait you can independently choose to give regardless of another person's behavior.

We have each been involved in numerous cases where respect was given even after less-than-desirable circumstances. For instance:

- After years of severe disappointment and hurt, a woman chooses to treat her husband's family without harshness or hate. (She established good boundaries as a way of maintaining her ability to respect.)

- A man disrespects his father's workaholism, yet when he speaks to him he refuses to let bitterness be his guide. He will be civil.

- A woman has been insulted by her sister because of disagreements regarding their parents' estate after their death. While she will hold firm in her convictions, she will choose not to succumb to a war of words, as her sister would readily do.

- A mother and father have been manipulated by their adult daughter. They have chosen consequences to maintain, yet they will not speak harshly or condemningly to her.

Can you see the general theme running through each of these illustrations? If the offended persons wanted a reason to act rudely or disrespectfully, they certainly had good excuses. Instead of lowering themselves to unbecoming behavior, though, they each chose to take the high road by maintaining respectful behavior even as they held firmly to their convictions.

The choice of respect does not require you to become a patsy or a pushover. Your respect for yourself will not allow that. Being respectful of others, you can choose to stay on course with traits you know will keep you on an emotionally stable track.

Consider your difficult experiences with people who have caused you harm. How could you choose to be respectful in spite of the painful feelings the other person brought to you? (For instance, "I could refrain from speaking insultingly about my friend who betrayed me," or "I could maintain politeness when I'm around my brother-in-law at family functions.")

How would the choice of respect help you in your healing process? (For instance, "It would remind me that I don't have to lower myself to crude behavior," or "I would feel released from the bitterness that has been so natural to me in the past.")

As Marcia considered the option of being respectful toward her father, she made a statement that neatly summarizes the challenge of many who face similar circumstances. "I've got to remember that *he* is not the one who sets my personal agenda. Who I am is an issue between myself and God, and I don't want my dad to cancel what I have decided in my heart is the best way to live."

Can you think like that? How can you hold firm in your choice to respect, even if the wrongdoer does not make it easy for you? (For instance, "I'll remind myself how pleasing it feels as I observe myself taking the high ground," or "My commitment to God will overshadow the temptation to act in ways I don't like.")

_____

_____

_____

Calm Confidence

When you forgive, choosing a commitment to the traits that are most mature and responsible, a calm confidence can come over you that sustains you and energizes you toward a continuation of the godly traits you prefer. When nonforgiveness persists, you are susceptible to insecurity because your emotions continue to be yanked around by the one who has harmed you. Though you can logically defend your reasons for feeling powerfully negative emotions, nonforgiveness leaves you feeling unconfident because of the undesirable nature of those negative emotions.

By committing to calm confidence you are affirming that your wrongdoer will not be the most powerful force in your life. That person will not be given the power of God to determine whether you can move forward with composure and inner peace.

Consider the statement made by Paul in Philippians 4:11, "I have learned in whatever state I am, to be content." That's powerful, and it can become your testimony.

What does contentment, or calm confidence, mean to you? (For instance, "It means I believe in myself even when others do not," or "My inner strength comes from a Source more powerful than anything humans can give.")

_____

_____

_____

As your wrongdoer chose to act negatively toward you, he or she was regrettably sending you the message, "I do not think highly of you." As you received that message, perhaps many times, your own confidence began to fade. Perhaps you thought, *Maybe there's something very wrong with me,* or *Did I do something to cause this awful thing to happen?*

How has your confidence been shaken through your difficult circumstances? (For instance, "I used to feel strong until my divorce, but now I don't like being seen by the old crowd," or "My mother has put me down so many times that I wonder if I make any decisions right.")

_____

_____

_____

Going back to the idea that all of us are dependent in some way, it is only natural that your inner confidence would be shaken when someone has rejected you. But keep a major thought in mind as you choose to sidestep the insecurity that might befall you: Though others were given the task to show you the way toward confidence, many have failed you by being rejecting or manipulative. That does not mean the message of devaluation is true. The truth of God's love is real in spite of people's failure to recognize it.

Marcia's greatest challenge was to keep logic ahead of her emotions. "You know, when I ask myself if my father's words should have more power over me than the Bible's words, the answer is extremely clear. My father is not a good representative of ultimate truth. But my problem with confidence stems from the fact that I've observed his rudeness toward me for so long that his message can win out because it has been given to me repeatedly."

Like Marcia, you will need to remember that inner calm is a by-product of a commitment to traits consistent with the direction you believe God has for you. If others choose to go along with your good choices, that's nice. If they do not, that's too bad. You can persist with the determination that you will not let misguided people determine your personal direction.

Consider how calm confidence can affect your behavior:

- You'll spend less time defending yourself. Why defend what needs no defense?

- When stating your boundaries or expressing legitimate anger, you can use a firm, yet noncoercive tone of voice.

- You will focus on what is good within yourself and live with those traits leading the way.

- You will focus on what is good in others, especially those who have been supportive of you. Words of thanks will flow easily.

- You will not react with surprise when wrong treatment does not abate.

- While enjoying the compliments given to you by others, you will not grope for compliments.

- If someone else wants to talk obsessively about the problems you have experienced, you will not feel the need to jump onto the bandwagon with self-pity or accusing words.

As you consider applying calm confidence in your lifestyle, how might it be demonstrated? (For instance, "When I'm around my mother-in-law, I will not feel the need to respond to her snippy comments about me," or "When in public, I'll not shrink from view when I encounter my ex-husband's business associates.")

_____

_____

_____

How can your determination to forgive be sustained by your commitment to calm confidence? (For instance, "In committing to confidence I realize that bitterness only reflects insecurity," or "I'll remind myself that I don't need the volatility that comes with an unforgiving spirit.")

_____

_____

_____

Resisting Vengeance

A fourth key trait in your mission toward forgiveness is resisting vengeance. Vengeance can be defined as a punishing spirit in the midst of wrongdoing. By suggesting that you resist vengeance we are not implying that the desire for fairness or appropriate discipline should be forfeited. Rather, we are suggesting that the application of ultimate punishment be handed over to God, not applied by you.

On many occasions we have witnessed how personalities can be negatively impacted because the requirement for vengeance has reached obsessive proportions. As examples:

- A man forced into bankruptcy by a dishonest business partner cannot say enough spiteful things in public about that partner. He becomes openly bitter and therefore ineffective with people.

- An entire extended family talks frequently and at great length about their former son-in-law, bitterly insisting that anyone who does not condemn him as they do should be shunned.

- A daughter who was the victim of her father's abuse wants other family members to have nothing to do with him, just as she has chosen to do.

- A young man who was jilted by his lover makes it his mission to ruin her reputation to anyone who will listen to his attacks on her character.

Did these people have reasonable causes to feel as negatively as they did? In most cases, yes. Did they find emotional healing as they clung to the need to punish their wrongdoer? Not at all. They made the mistake of listening to the message of justice demanded by their pain without also counting the cost of the additional pain brought on by a vengeful spirit.

In what circumstance have you struggled with a vengeful spirit? (For instance, "When I saw my former friend being buddies with some of my other friends I wanted to scream because she was acting so phony," or "My ex-husband was physically abusive but he has never had to answer to anyone in his church about his treatment of women.")

_____

_____

_____

What makes vengeance so tempting is the possibility that the wrongdoer may get off scot-free from consequences unless you make a major issue of his or her sins. What penalties would you like to see given to your wrongdoer? (For instance, "I don't think my abusive mother should have the status of a loving grandmother to all of my siblings' kids," or "I think my ex-husband should be dismissed from the church committees he is on.")

_____

_____

_____

There are times when it can be appropriate to establish consequences or tell your side of the story when a wrongdoer seems intent on living a perfectly charmed life, experiencing no consequences for the wrongs committed. In situations when it is responsible for you to speak the truth about your pain, do so. An example would be a mother of an adult son who had to tell him about her brother's past manipulation because it appeared the brother was about to talk her son into a joint business venture. Her open statements about her hurt did not reveal a vengeful spirit, but a loving response to her son.

Be willing to incorporate boundaries and assertions as part of your healing process (as discussed in Chapters 2 and 4), yet also remember that you are limited in the ability to insist on fair consequences at all times. In some circumstances, your limits may require you to witness wrongdoers experiencing only mild repercussion (if any at all) for their wrongs. It will not be easy to accept such unfairness, yet your limitations may prevent you from making every wrong right.

Can you live within the boundaries of your limits? What limits will you need to accept as you commit to resisting vengeance? (For instance, "I am limited in making my sister have a well-developed conscience," or "My former friend cuts off anyone who speaks truth, including me.")

_____

_____

_____

Scripture reminds us that God will not let wrongs go eternally unchallenged. In His justice He will see that discipline and punishment are fairly managed. Consider Hebrews 10:30–31: "For we know Him who said, 'Vengeance is Mine; I will repay,' says the Lord. And again, 'The LORD will judge His people.' It is a fearful thing to fall into the hands of the living God."

We cannot possibly understand God's timing or His methods of exacting vengeance, but the message is clear: God is in control, you are not. Accept that.

As you step away from attempts to exact vengeance, you can stay on your mission to let more pleasing traits dominate your personality. You will not be required to deny your legitimate hurt, rather you can let go of the illusion of controlling others knowing that God is in control. You are then free to expend your energy on emotionally healthy goals.

What commitment will you make to yourself as you let go of your need for vengeance? (For instance, "I will cease my campaign to ruin my sister-in-law's reputation," or "I will stop my open accusations toward my father since he doesn't listen anyway.")

_____

_____

_____

Remember, your mission is to be as emotionally healthy as possible. Your commitment to love, respect, embrace calm confidence, and resist vengeance is an extension of your commitment to your own emotional and spiritual stability.

In the next chapter we will explore the most important trait of all in your quest to be a forgiving person. We will examine how your own humility will help you come to terms with the pride exhibited by others.

11

Embracing Humility

Step 11. Come to terms with others' wrong deeds by recognizing your own need for forgiveness.

At the core of every personality is the characteristic of pride, the preoccupation with one's own desires and preferences. No one is immune; we all have it in one form or another.

Think of the many ways pride is evidenced. When persons are critical, for instance, it is propelled by self-preoccupied thoughts about how they think the world should be. Likewise, when persons are easily hurt and offended it can be fed by the inner insistence that they should receive preferred treatment. Or consider that impatience is fueled by the insistence that events should proceed with one's own timing given greater priority. Insensitive words, a judgmental spirit, aloofness, a lack of concern, open aggression, sexual deviance, each of these traits in their own way reflects a self-absorbed attitude, an unwillingness to consider the needs of others.

Where does the prideful spirit come from? It is not learned, though experiences can certainly give shape to the eventual forms pride will take. Pride is inborn, it is natural to human nature. It is at the heart of each person's sinfulness. That is why it is so widespread, and that is why it cannot be avoided.

To get an idea of the naturalness of pride, observe the behavior of a one-year-old baby. Do you have to teach that child to be self-centered? To throw temper tantrums? To ignore the pleas of parents? To make demands on the spot? Not at all. These traits, which reflect pride, are indigenous to that child's character. There is no need for us to think harshly toward little children because they do not know better. Our point is that they exhibit a preoccupation with self before they can be taught anything else.

When does this quality dissolve and cease to be? It doesn't, at least not on this side of heaven.

Now, think about the painful circumstances you have experienced because of others' mistreatment of you. Can you see how the wrongdoer was driven by pride? Your pain was the direct result of another person's need to put selfish needs above all else.

In what way does your pain reflect the pride of the wrongdoer? (For instance, "My marriage broke up because my spouse did not want to make the personal sacrifices necessary," or "My uncle who abused me could think only about his desires for the moment, not mine.")

_____

_____

_____

There is no way to get around it, pride will be demonstrated toward you by many people in your life for as long as you live. It is ugly and it is unavoidable. Listed here are just a few of the ways our patients have been hurt because of others' pride. Perhaps you can relate to some of them:

- A wife pleads with her husband to help discipline the kids fairly, not angrily. He responds by saying he will do what he wants to do, and she should butt out.

- An adult son wants to make peace with his mother, but she will hear none of his concerns.

- Two sisters cannot attend the same family functions because one had a sexual fling with the other's boyfriend.

- A supervisor has chronic problems at work because a subordinate continues to sabotage his authority.

- A husband lives in chronic misery because his wife will not give up her alcohol abuse.

- Parents agonize because their son refuses to respond to treatment for drug use.

- A woman endures intense loneliness because her friend "backstabbed" her with a group of women.

- A wife dreads the Christmas holidays because her mother-in-law is so finicky and controlling.

In each instance you can see how the person's pain was a direct by-product of the other person's pride. In each case, the pain was deepened by the wrongdoer's unwillingness to admit the problem.

Let's revisit Daniel, the recovering alcoholic who also had strains with his parents because of their inability to admit their contribution to the family problems. "I don't mean to play the blame game," he once told Dr. Minirth, "but as I learn more about the healthier side of life I can't help but think about how my life would have been a lot smoother if my parents had been less concerned about their own agendas and more tuned in to my legitimate needs. The problems I'm having with them now are not at all new."

"What do you mean?"

"I remember as a kid how I constantly felt I was a bother to my parents, that they had plans and preferences that didn't include me. When I was in the sixth grade I was a good little baseball player and wanted to play in an organized league, but I wasn't allowed to do so. My mother said she didn't want to have to schedule dinner around my practices, and she felt the fifteen-dollar entry fee was too expensive."

"How did you respond to that?"

"Well, like any twelve-year-old kid, I pleaded my case. I knew we could work out some compromises, and I was willing to do whatever it took to keep my time requirements balanced. But as I talked with my parents about my preferences I remember wondering to myself why I should waste my breath. It was a rare day that I felt they cared about me. I know kids can be selfish and demanding, but I honestly believe that at that point in my life I was truly a team player. I remember *many* other episodes where I felt that my parents just thought about their own preferences. My brother says he feels the same way."

Recall that Daniel felt burdened by his extended family when in his mid-forties he openly admitted his problem with alcohol. He told Dr. Minirth that the judgment and criticism brought on by his admission were nothing new. He had felt for years that he had to tread carefully around his parents because he never knew when the criticism would come.

Were Daniel's problems compounded by his parents' preoccupation with themselves? Yes. We cannot say for sure that he would have been able to avoid his problems had his parents been more approachable or understanding, but it is safe to say that their pride issues did not help Daniel.

Likewise, you can probably see clearly where another person's self-centeredness played a major role in your pain. Hardly any interpersonal conflict is void of this ugly quality. You are normal, just as Daniel was, to declare how strongly you do not like that trait in others. You are also normal to admit that the other person's pride makes forgiveness a less-than-natural response from you.

Admitting Your Own Pride

Now let's examine the harder subject. While your wrongdoers have exhibited pride, often to the gross extreme, you, too, have this characteristic within your personality. Perhaps your pride did not play a role in the events that caused your pain, but perhaps it did. Either way, as you confess your own inclination toward self-preoccupation you may conclude that it would be inappropriate to harbor a grudge toward someone when you also have qualities that are less than perfect.

Admitting your own pride can be difficult because you do not want to think that you are on the same low level as the one who harmed you. As we explore your own propensity toward this trait, let's be clear to affirm that your pain is legitimate. Likewise, we are not going to put you on a comparative scale with the wrongdoer, concluding that you are as awful as anyone else. That's not our intent. Instead, as you recognize your own ability to be imperfect, as you realize your own need for forgiveness, you will be more capable of giving others forgiveness.

Recall Jesus' parable of forgiveness as recorded in Matthew 18:23–35. A servant's very large debt was forgiven by the master, yet when the servant was in a position to forgive someone else, he would not. The master became very angry and forced the servant to repay his large debt since he would not forgive just as he had been forgiven. Christ's message is clear. We are all in the same boat in the sense that we each need forgiveness in some form. It is not fair to ask God to forgive us when we choose not to forgive others.

Are you willing to admit that you, too, can be prideful and insensitive to others? Such an admission need not be accompanied by self-judgment or hatred. We are only seeking honesty. Let's take a look at some examples of people who had to make concessions regarding their own imperfections:

- A woman recalls how insensitive her father was when she was a girl and how it produced much pain and insecurity in her. Yet she also had to admit that she, too, could be blunt and insensitive toward her three kids.

- A divorced husband is bitter about the way his ex-wife speaks about him behind his back, but he also knows he has been less than flattering in the way he has talked about her.

- A friend feels slighted because his friend has not been consistent in keeping commitments, yet he recognizes that sometimes he, too, thinks about only his own preferences.

- A woman realizes her friend lied to her, which hurts deeply. Yet she, too, has been less than honest at times.

- A man despises his brother's loud, abusive, and angry outbursts. He cannot remember being openly abusive like his brother, but he knows he can irritate people with his long, silent withdrawals.

Perhaps your sins do not appear to be as severe as the ones committed by those who have harmed you. Nonetheless, you *do* have pockets of sin for which you, too, need forgiveness.

What flaws do you see in yourself that reflect a self-preoccupation or an insensitivity toward others? (For instance, "I struggle regularly with a critical spirit," or "I've never had an affair like my spouse, yet I'm fully capable of lust.")

As you confess your own need for forgiveness you can conclude that you are in no position to be nonforgiving. That realization caused Daniel to become very introspective. "You know, I like to think that I've made a few steps forward as compared to some of the traits my parents have," he told Dr. Minirth. "As I recall how they did not include me in many decisions as a boy, I have been determined to be much fairer with Brian as we discuss how his needs can be handled by our family."

Dr. Minirth smiled. "So even though you didn't have good communication in your home, you used your past experiences to motivate you to be a better communicator now. I like that!"

"I could really stand up and crow if it were true that I've turned all my family's negatives into positives, but you know that's not how the story ends. I look back on my twenties and thirties when I did most of my heavy drinking and I realize that I was no saint. I'd hate to have to count the number of times when I just wasn't there for Belinda or I just ignored Brian's needs. All the money I wasted, all the time that I lost, took a toll on my wife and son."

"You're feeling guilt about your past," said Dr. Minirth, "and even though I want you to be able to put it behind you, it's not completely wrong for you to feel guilty."

"I thought psychiatrists always tried to teach people not to have guilt!"

"I can't speak for all psychiatrists," said Dr. Minirth, "but I can tell you I'd hate for you to have no guilt. That would be awful. Certainly you don't need to be ruled by guilt, but you need *some* because it can keep you from being too prideful."

What about you? Can you, like Daniel, learn that guilt can be part of your healing? What is good about some of your feelings of guilt? (For instance, "It keeps me from being judgmental toward others," or "It reminds me that because I need others to be gracious toward me, I, too, should be a giver of grace.")

The greatest result of your sense of guilt can be the development of humility. As this trait gains a foothold in your personality, you will be much farther down the road toward personal wholeness.

Embracing Humility

"When you consider the word *humble* what first comes to mind?" That's the question Dr. Minirth posed to Daniel as they discussed his reaction to his parents.

"In the past I used to think a humble person was just a pushover. You know, if someone else comes on strong, the humble person just lies down, giving no resistance."

"That could leave a lot of tire marks on your body," said the doctor.

"In the last few years I've developed a much deeper appreciation for humility," said Daniel. "I've realized that I need it in large doses, and it seems to bring out the good in me."

How about you? What is your understanding of the meaning of humility? (For instance, "It's not really necessary," or "It means being a servant.")

Dr. Minirth told Daniel, "To get an idea of what godly humility is, think about it in opposite terms of pride. Whereas pride reflects a preoccupation with self, humility can consider the perspective of others. If pride is self-serving, humility is God-serving. Since pride implies a need to be in control, humility realizes personal limits and that control is not always possible."

Daniel's mind was clicking as the doctor challenged him to rethink humility's definition. In time he came to realize that forgiveness could only come as he was committed to a deep sense of humility.

To get an idea of your readiness for humility, check the following statements that could apply to you:

— I can handle the fact that the world does not owe me favored treatment.
— Though it is reasonable to try to avoid pain, I am wise enough to know I can't avoid it altogether.
— When I am assertive I do it because I care, not because I am just being pushy.
— I feel sorrow for others' problems, even toward those who have done me wrong.
— I have very little desire to exert power over others.
— While vengeance may feel temporarily satisfying, it seems empty to live for vengeance.
— I can acknowledge that other people have the prerogative to be wrong, and it is not always my job to correct them.
— I would much rather live as an encourager than a critic. I'm committed to this.
— When someone wants to persuade me to their position, it's not necessarily my place to make them see the error in their thinking. I can stay out of circular arguments.
— Admitting my own imperfections helps me forgive others of theirs.

Each statement implies a form of humility, so the more you were able to check, the more likely you will be to accept what is right about humility. If you checked eight or more, it is very likely you are on the right path.

Daniel spoke very candidly with Dr. Minirth. "In my early adult years I didn't put two minutes of thought into the subject of humility. Occasionally I might hear a minister mention something about it, but it just didn't interest me at all. But that's changed a lot in the past few years."

"Problems have a way of bringing out the philosopher in you, and that's not all that bad," said Dr. Minirth. "If you *didn't* think deeply about your guiding beliefs at a time like this, that would be cause for concern."

"You know, the greatest aggravation that faces me now is that neither my mother nor my father seems interested in taking the hard look inside that would prove so helpful. It would certainly make my healing a lot easier if they would join me in personal exploration. And to some extent, Belinda also is lagging behind in her willingness to humble herself through self-examination. She's admitted some of the ways she's contributed to our marital problems, yet she also will let me take on more than half the blame."

The problem Daniel expressed is not at all uncommon, nor was it necessarily wrong of him to wish that these people would join him in embracing humility. After all, the improvements made by key people in your life can certainly make your efforts more satisfying.

What efforts toward humility would you like to see in the wrong-doers in your life? (For instance, "I'd love it if my dad would admit how hardheaded he is and how his stubbornness could be eliminated," or "I wish my judgmental friends would tell me how they realized it was wrong to think of me in condemning terms.")

_____

_____

_____

How would your ability to forgive be enhanced by such humility in others? (For instance, "I'd be much more patient with my dad on the occasions he slipped back into his old bad habits," or "It would help me feel more secure if my friends would admit their contributions to our problems.")

_____

_____

_____

If there is a possibility that the others in your life could listen to your thoughts about joining you in embracing humility, be assertive and make it a matter of open discussion and planning. Be specific in what you would like to see from them and what they could expect from you.

For instance, Daniel knew his wife, Belinda, was open-minded about psychological and spiritual matters. Part of the reason she had not joined him in personal growth was due to Daniel's hesitance to discuss with her some of his counseling insights. "In the past," he explained, "I spent so much time telling her it was her fault when I had problems that I was afraid to give her the impression that I'm still thinking like that. I figured some time needed to pass so I could *show* her that I'm serious about being responsible for my own actions rather than giving the impression she'd better change with me."

"I respect that reasoning," said Dr. Minirth. "I respect it a lot. And because of that, I think you now have a foundation of credibility to build upon with Belinda."

Daniel and Belinda decided to take no fewer than two or three times per week to discuss ways they wanted to see each other adjust and improve. They decided to study books together so their discussions could stay focused and purposeful. In doing so, both showed humility since each approached their discussion with the thought, *I know I need to improve, and I'm willing to learn how.*

Daniel's parents were a different story. Recall from Chapter 8 that he attempted to confront them constructively with the intent to smooth over conflicts that had been brewing regarding their treatment of Daniel's son, Brian. Not only did they not want to hear Daniel's concerns, but pride caused them to deny their negatives. The result was an increasingly superficial relationship with him.

What factors do you see in the people you've had conflict with that tell you if they can or cannot incorporate humility with you? (For instance, "My brother has shown greater interest in spiritual growth, which is a good sign," or "My mother-in-law is incredibly defensive regarding any personal matter.")

_____

_____

_____

Whether your wrongdoers will or will not join you, are you ready to remove your own pockets of pride and move more deeply into a life of humility? How would you describe your attitude about this? (For instance, "I'm ready to develop humility because I just don't need the bitterness that accompanies pride," or "I'm hesitant, but at least I'll keep an open mind.")

_____

_____

_____

What aspects of pride will you focus on first? (For instance, "I'm ready to drop my judgments against those who have judged me," or "I realize that it is prideful for me to speak so sarcastically about my stepfather, even though he is an unpleasant man. I'm ready to give that sarcasm up.")

_____

_____

_____

God's Mercy over You

Christ taught that your willingness to forgive will be in direct proportion to your recognition of your need to be forgiven (Matt. 5:7; Rom. 5:7–8; Eph. 2:4–5). Not one of us can stand on our own before God and declare, "Well, here I am, Lord! Aren't You fortunate to have me on Your side!" That would be the ultimate in pride.

God is under no obligation to contend with sin or sinners. In fact, He is the embodiment of holiness, meaning He is so other than us, so set apart, that our ways do not come close to approaching His ways (Isa. 55:8). When Adam and Eve chose the path of sin it was God's perfect right to terminate any and all contact with humanity from that point on. Our preoccupation with self is an incredible affront to Him since it causes us to worship ourselves, not Him. It prompts us to consider first our own preferences, not His. The very fact that He extends Himself to us as He does is miraculous. It is not to be taken lightly.

One of the amazing features of heaven surely will be the ecstasy that will come over each of us as we fully realize the grandeur of His deity as compared to the lowliness of our humanity. We will surely break out in songs with the angels as we think of nothing less than praising Him for choosing life with us. The message of Christ can be summarized by the thought that God loves so deeply that He chose to do whatever it took to communicate that love, even if it meant giving Himself completely for us.

Mercy is defined as the giving of love and favor where it is not merited or earned. In fact, it is given in the place of the rejection or punishment that *is* deserved.

Do you acknowledge that you have no right to ask for favor from God for your shortcomings? Are you aware that God suspends His demands for perfection in order to give you His love? Do you realize that if you are a believer in Christ's substitutionary death on your behalf that God will see you in the same perfect light in which He sees Christ? That's the gospel message of salvation. That's mercy!

What understanding do you have of the mercy God offers you? (For instance, "I am forever grateful for God's acceptance of me as one of His very own," or "I want to believe in His mercy, but it seems almost too good to be true.")

_____

_____

_____

Your heartfelt gratitude for the mercy of God will be the single most important ingredient in your journey to offer forgiveness toward others. As you claim that mercy, you will want to give it to others. If you feel you have no need for mercy, you likely will not feel compelled to offer it to those who have wronged you.

Dr. Minirth spoke reflectively with Daniel. "We've covered a lot of ground since you first came into counseling. At first our concerns centered around getting your life straightened out in the aftermath of your problems with alcohol abuse and financial burdens. You've done much to take responsibility for your errors, and because of that you're a real inspiration to me.

"As you've steadily gained insight you've realized that not all is well with people in your extended family, particularly your mother and father. You've addressed your problems fairly with them, and though they haven't responded as you would like, at least you've cleared the air of some major problems that have been laying dormant for years. I'm impressed by the fact that God has His hand on you. He's guiding you toward a better way of life, and because of your responsiveness to Him, it's showing major results."

Daniel received those words appreciatively. "You know, when I look at the ways I've made a mess of my life, how I've put Belinda and Brian through all sorts of agony, it's a wonder that God would have anything to do with me. I really have to stop often to count my blessings."

"As disappointed as you've felt regarding your parents' lack of awareness," Dr. Minirth reflected, "I'm hoping you can choose to extend the same grace to them that God has extended to you. Part of the definition of grace and mercy is that it's offered where it is not earned."

Daniel was receptive. "Who am I to hold myself over anyone? I've received forgiveness when it was not deserved. Surely I can turn around and give it away."

Think about your own inadequacies and mistakes. How has God shown mercy to you? (For instance, "In my early adult years I was promiscuous, yet God does not hold that against me now," or "I've been prone to phoniness, yet God sees through it and loves me in spite of it.")

_____

_____

_____

Focus on Your Thanks Toward God

As you remind yourself that you have been given God's mercy your heart can be filled with thanksgiving. You can train yourself to focus on what is good in your life rather than on what is awful. A good verse to guide you is Philippians 4:8: "Whatever things are true, whatever things are noble, whatever things are just, whatever things are pure, whatever things are lovely, whatever things are of good report, if there is any virtue and if there is anything praiseworthy— meditate on these things."

Daniel was challenged to a unique exercise based on Philippians 4:8. Rather than just nodding as he read this verse then thinking, *This is a fine verse,* he was challenged to take each component of it and write what corresponded with it in his life:

- True: It is true that I am a sinner saved by grace. My future with God is secure.

- Noble: I have a commitment to my marriage and to my role as father. I will not take these lightly.

- Just: The Golden Rule is best. I will treat others as I would have them treat me.

- Pure: Kindness is one of the purest acts I can do, it can be given with no worry about the return.

- Lovely: My love for Belinda is amazing. I am blessed to have her as my wife.

- Of Good Report: I admire Brian for the way he tries to be a standard-bearer among his college friends.

- Excellence: The ethics I see in my brother are excellent. He is a trustworthy person.

- Worthy of Praise: I'll praise God for His constant love for me.

After finishing his assignment, which was done with great contemplation, Daniel admitted, "I've read that verse before and, of course, I always agree with it, but it's only been nice sounding words. Putting specifics to each part of it makes me realize how I need to be reminded repeatedly of the good things in my life."

Would you be willing to go through the same exercise? In the space provided, write about the things in your life that would correspond to each of the traits mentioned.

- True:

- Noble:

- Just:

- Pure:

- Lovely:

- Of Good Report:

- Excellence:

- Worthy of Praise:

Now, notice the effect of a thankful spirit on your emotions. While you cannot take away the memories of the aggravations you have felt, you can be reminded that there are some good things to sustain you. In humility you can let go of your demand for all things to be perfect, yet you can focus on the reality that there is an upbeat mind-set that can guide you.

As you remind yourself of the things that are good, how does that help you in the ability to forgive? (For instance, "It reminds me that I need not waste too much emotional energy thinking only about the lousy stuff in my life," or "It makes me want to be upbeat more frequently.")

_____

_____

_____

Separating from Others' Pride

By clinging to nonforgiveness you are letting the pridefulness of others dominate. In essence, you are responding to pride with pride, leaving you still attached to the wrongdoer. That person is still pulling your strings.

Choosing humility, however, is your declaration that you want no further entanglement with the wrongs committed against you. You will be affirming your commitment to a more productive way of life, one anchored in God's traits, not the traits of imperfect people.

As you develop an awareness of the enormous difference between pride and humility, there are three patterns of pride you will want to be aware of: the pride of unbelief, Pharisaism, and grace abuse. Perhaps you will notice how your wrongdoers fit into one or more of these categories. If you do, you can (1) feel pity for them, and (2) you can choose not to succumb to these patterns yourself. Let's look at each.

1. The Pride of Unbelief

The Bible tells us that each person has some level of God awareness (see Rom. 1:18–20). At some point in every person's life there is a day of reckoning regarding obedience to God. No mature adult can say, "I had no idea I was supposed to make a decision about my belief in God."

Some people have chosen not to give God a place in their lives. They have concluded that He simply is irrelevant, so they will move forward making decisions based on their own understanding of what should be. These people see themselves as sufficiently capable of being gods unto themselves. When this is the case, the potential is strong that they will allow ungodly habits or attitudes to predominate. Having no allegiance to God, they can be more susceptible to manipulation, insensitivity, rejection, abusiveness, nonforgiveness, and the like.

Who in your life has shown tendencies to exhibit the pride that accompanies unbelief? (For instance, "My brother couldn't care less about God, and in doing so he lives for whatever makes him happy at the moment," or "My parents are unbelievers, and whereas they aren't blatantly immoral, neither are they fully capable of love.")

How would compassion toward unbelievers help you to forgive? (For instance, "I would sadly realize my brother has no compass to guide him," or "I would not expect my parents to know how to respond to me since they have not truly contemplated the implications of God's love.")

_____

_____

_____

Now, here is the harder question. When in your life have you lived with the pride of an unbeliever? (For instance, "In my teens my Christian beliefs were not really my own, and I was easily given to temper outbursts," or "Prior to my conversion, I lived a party lifestyle, unconcerned about others' needs.")

_____

_____

_____

As you remember your own unbelief, how can this keep you anchored in forgiveness and grace? (For instance, "How can I not forgive when I've needed it so badly?" or "I can empathize with my brother because I used to be the same way.")

_____

_____

_____

2. The Pride of Pharisaism

In the biblical days, the Pharisees professed a deep devotion to God, yet their obsession with rules and correct performance blinded them from knowing and living the love of God. Today, many churches are filled with people who fit the same profile. Some of these modern Pharisees may actually be believers who are, unfortunately, guided by misplaced emphases and priorities. Others are not Christians at all but simply committed to religious rules and regulations.

The most distinguishing elements of Pharisaism are a judgmental spirit and an insistence upon doing things exactly as they say in the name of religious correctness. Often these people believe they have such special wisdom from God that they do not need to listen to anyone with a differing perspective. As a result, they can be condescending, argumentative, stubborn, smug, critical, unbending, and bossy.

Who in your life has exhibited Pharisaical pride toward you? (For instance, "My husband disciplines the kids with a holier-than-thou attitude and expects me to fall in line as well," or "My former friend cannot accept my flawed life because I don't fit her mold.")

_____

_____

_____

How has your encounter with Pharisaism hindered your forgiveness? (For instance, "I hate it when I see my husband act so righteously; I have lots of bitterness," or "Who does my former friend think she is lording over me and my mistakes? I become sarcastic toward her.")

_____

_____

_____

Okay, another hard question. When have you ever acted with Pharisaism? (For instance, "I used to judge people who were divorced," or "I used to ignore neighbors who were not on the same page spiritually with me.")

_____

_____

_____

You cannot force others to give up their prideful Pharisaism, but you can set yours aside. As you embrace the humility this would require, how could you also be more forgiving? (For instance, "There is no need for me to hold others to my preferred standards when I can't even live up to them," or "I'll remember that my salvation has nothing to do with my being religiously correct, so I won't require that of others.")

3. The Pride of Grace Abusers

A third manifestation of pride is through grace abuse. Most people in this category have a saving understanding of Christ's work on their behalf, but instead of living with grateful submission to His ways, they take liberties to do things they clearly know to be wrong. "Hey, if I'm forgiven," the reasoning goes, "then it won't matter in the long run if I cut some corners here and there."

A cornerstone trait in the healthy Christian life is freedom, as opposed to a mind of regulatory duty. The grace abuser loves to focus on freedom but does not like giving too much thought to such balancing qualities as responsibility, submission, servitude, or self-restraint. Most will reason that they have tried those things only to find them stifling for one reason or another. As a result of their imbalanced use of freedom they can be prone to manipulation, irresponsibility, impulsiveness, shallow commitments, and excuse making. This can create great stress in you as you try to contend with them over the course of a long relationship.

When have you experienced strain due to someone else's grace abuse? (For instance, "When my husband decided to have an affair," or "My sister doesn't see the need to be discrete about her more permissive social habits when she is with my children.")

_____

_____

_____

How has another's grace abuse hindered your ability to forgive? (For instance, "I keep telling myself that my husband knows better than to let a seductive woman influence him," or "I resent my sister for being too hang-loose.")

_____

_____

_____

One more hard question. When have you ever abused grace? (For instance, "I rationalize my bitterness by saying I know God understands," or "I've had my moments when I've gone along with questionable social habits.")

_____

_____

_____

As you realize your own capability to pridefully abuse grace, how can you get closer to being the forgiving person God wants you to be? (For instance, "I'll hold firmly to my convictions with my husband, yet I'll also recognize that he can learn from his mistakes," or "I'll ease up on my critical spirit toward my sister.")

_____

_____

_____

As Daniel spoke with Dr. Minirth about the many implications of setting aside pride in favor of humility he concluded, "If I wanted to list all the legitimate reasons I have to hold grudges against my parents, I could come up with a fairly long list. But then as I look at my own history of mistakes and selfishness it seems pretty pointless for me to think of myself in haughty or conceited terms. I wish I could have a deeper understanding with them about what we could still enjoy as they grow older, but at this point it doesn't seem that will happen. My disappointment about the shallowness of our relationship, though, still gives me no excuse to hold grudges. I'll forgive because it makes perfect sense."

Perhaps you can conclude, like Daniel, that your own imperfect life prevents you from keeping score against those who have evidenced imperfection toward you. The humility that will accompany such a conclusion will keep you in a place of contentment as you realize you are becoming a living imitation of Christ.

In the next (and final) chapter we will build on the attitude of humility by examining the necessity of developing a spirit of encouragement. By giving of yourself to those who need it, you will be less inclined to remain stuck in the bitterness that accompanies nonforgiveness.

12

Becoming an Encourager

Step 12. Become a source of encouragement to other hurting people.

How many times have you heard someone say, "I learned the deepest truths about life during the periods when everything was absolutely terrific"? Probably not often. Now, how many times have you heard, "My most significant personal growth came after a period of great stress and difficulty"? That is far more common. Pain and disappointment, while hardly desirable, can cause people to search as never before for the truths that will sustain and guide them. It is said that the strongest, most durable oak trees are the ones that grow in forests pounded by severe storms and winds. The storm-beaten tree is forced to develop a deep and strong root system in order to withstand the elements. So it can be with humans. Exposure to pain and difficulty, though never pleasant, can create an inner strength that would otherwise not be produced.

Mark, the man who had strained relations with his adult daughters, Brianna and Laurie, had never been accused of being the philosophic type. "My mother always said 'keep it simple,'" he told Dr. Carter. "I never really enjoyed debates or discussions about psychological or theological principles. I've always assumed that if you try to live right, good things will eventually happen. Why go on and on about concepts and theories and ideas? It always seemed like wasted talk before now."

His voice became somber as he continued. "But this whole ordeal with Brianna and Laurie has thrown me into a time of questioning and groping that is very unusual for me. Here I am almost fifty years old, and I'm just now searching to find a philosophy that will keep me going strong."

In his discussions with Dr. Carter about his controlling nature, Mark had been convicted of the need to examine his guiding principles as never before, and he was enjoying the challenge, if not the circumstances. "You know, I'd never have thought that I'd need counseling. I mean, I've always been my own person, and I pretty much kept my inner thoughts to myself. But this whole experience has broadened my horizons in ways I'd never have suspected before."

"Aside from the adjustments you've made with your daughters, how are you changing?"

"The biggest change is that I'm noticing the feelings and needs of other people like never before. My wife, Mary Dana, says she's been amazed that I'll slow down to talk with people about personal matters. In the past, I've been a 'strictly business' sort of guy, and I'm still that way a lot of the time. But because of my frustrations, and maybe my age has something to do with it, I'm realizing that there's a great need for people to connect on a less superficial level."

He then described to Dr. Carter how he had befriended a man who also was experiencing strains with his grown kids. "I let him talk about his miseries, and I shared with him a few of my own. In years past I wouldn't have given two seconds of thought about someone else's personal life. Before now I always assumed it was none of my business if someone else had problems."

Never would Mark have wished for the problems he had with his girls. As Dr. Carter once said to him, "When you were twenty years old, if you had been asked to map out the way you expected your life to unfold, you certainly wouldn't have included the problems of divorce and broken communication with your children. Nonetheless, that's what's happened. That's your reality."

Mark had realized he could choose where to go from here, and he had chosen a path that included more emphasis on personal relating skills and a strengthened spiritual life. "Strange isn't it," he said, "that my bottom had to fall out before I could grow."

Think back on your difficult circumstances. How have they caused you to make personal improvements? (For instance, "I've been forced to retool my mind to include less judgment," or "My split with my dad has caused me to question my real beliefs about my heavenly Father.")

_____

_____

_____

Never Be Threatened by a Crisis

If you could choose, you would have no crises. Life would be a bed of roses, meaning you would find success and acceptance at every turn. Wouldn't that be nice! Yet, that is not reality. You have felt the anguish that accompanies rejection. You have been severely disappointed. People have let you down, or perhaps they have even harmed you and treated you cruelly. Nothing can change these facts now.

As we have treated thousands of people through the past decades we have determined that you can place those who have suffered humiliation into one of two categories: (1) Those who remain perpetually stuck in the problems created by circumstances, and (2) Those who optimistically assume they can use the lessons learned from problems to propel them toward growth and wisdom.

Into which category do you fit?

In the past, how have you been tempted to give up because of emotional manipulation or rejection? (For instance, "Because of my broken relationships with the men in my family I've felt as though I should just write off any possibility of having good relationships with males," or "After losing my closest friend I gave up nearly all of my social activities.")

_____

_____

_____

Let's affirm that it is normal to grieve when you have experienced loss, yet let's also be aware that your emotions can carry you toward lifestyle extremes that ultimately work against you. Be aware of your capacity to let difficulties ruin you.

Now shift gears. How can your past problems be used to spur personal growth? (For instance, "Because of my history of poor relationships with men I've learned to communicate with clear boundaries," or "My broken relationship with my closest friend compels me to have deeper honesty now in my other meaningful relationships.")

_____

_____

_____

As Dr. Carter spoke with Mark about his newfound interest in personal soul-searching he reflected, "It really is regrettable that things have not worked out as planned with your daughters, yet I'm detecting that you're not going to let this problem get the best of you."

"That's my hope. I feel like I've made some mistakes with them through the years, so I've got to determine that those mistakes will motivate me to approach current and future relationships differently. Common sense tells me not to sit comfortably with my old style of relating. Since pain came out of it, it seems that I should be making some major improvements."

"I've always believed you should never be threatened by a crisis," said Dr. Carter. "While a crisis can produce great pain, it can also prompt tremendous growth. I'd like to see that happen with you."

When writing about his "thorn in the flesh" the apostle Paul illustrated how he had chosen to turn a negative into a great positive. He admitted pleading with God to remove his problem, but to no avail. In time (surely this did not happen overnight) he realized God had something more in mind for him. Paul wrote, "And He said to me, 'My grace is sufficient for you, for My strength is made perfect in weakness'" (2 Cor. 12:9).

Your pain may not be felt in the form of a physical ailment as Paul's probably was, yet you, too, can receive the same healing message from God. Through your difficulties God's grace can be shown. Most likely you will realize that because people and circumstances will fail you, God's grace is all you have left to turn to. He alone is dependable; people are not.

How can you turn your difficult circumstances into a lesson that shows you the grace of God? (For instance, "When I was at my lowest point a friend showed me true compassion. I can see this as a God-given gift," or "Because of my hardship with my mother I'm much more compassionate toward people who hurt. This is God working in my life.")

Let's take Paul's passage one step farther. Not only did he realize God's grace would come upon him in the midst of his weakness, he actually determined not to be threatened by further problems: "Therefore I take pleasure in infirmities, in reproaches, in needs, in persecutions, in distresses, for Christ's sake. For when I am weak, then I am strong" (2 Cor. 12:10). Powerful words! His conclusions are far different from the ones drawn by most. Again let's underscore that you do not have to become a masochist to embrace Paul's words. It's not wrong to avoid pain where possible. But in the event of pain, you can choose to move forward, not backward.

If you chose to be less threatened by your crisis, how would your outlook on life improve? (For instance, "I'd realize that in spite of my parents' rigidity I can develop my own flexible manner of dealing with people," or "My experience of rejection will not defeat me because I know now what priorities will help me have a fuller life.")

_____

_____

_____

When Mark realized he could not enjoy the desired relationship with his adult daughters, a brokenness came over him that he had never experienced before. "This is just not right," he had lamented. "I never wanted things to turn out this way. Two of the happiest days of my life were the days when Brianna and Laurie were born. I was just ecstatic! Now it's come to this." He just shook his head sadly.

"So where do you go from here?"

"I've got nowhere to go but up. I may have lost my chance with those two, although it's still too soon to say I've given up on them. But I still have my teenage son and I have my wife. Without question, things will be different, for the better."

"You recently said that you've befriended a man with similar family problems. Could I assume that your manner of relating to him will bring out a different dimension in your personality?"

"Absolutely. In the past I kept personal matters strictly to myself, but now I'm much more willing to be open. What's the point of having friends if you can't share who you are with each other?"

Can you see what was happening to Mark? Originally, he sought counseling because he needed to come to terms with his daughters. Wisely he learned to monitor his emotions and his relational style more carefully. Now he was learning to be more successful in his current relationships. His brokenness was a key ingredient in his growth.

Once you get beyond the trauma of your painful experiences, you, too, can become a bright spot among family and friends. Realistically, some people will not want to relate with you in an improved manner. Instead, they may continue to fall back on worn and weary patterns. If that is the case, choose to move forward anyway. Whether or not they acknowledge it, you have much to offer in spite of (or perhaps we should say *because* of) your undesirable circumstances. Start looking for ways to establish yourself as a positive presence in the lives of people who *can* receive what you have to offer.

To determine if you are ready to become a more encouraging presence toward others, check each of the following statements that would apply to you:

— I am much less inclined than in the past to be a critic. I look for what is right.
— My frustrating experiences have taught me the value of patience.
— I feel that I can sense more readily when a person is in need of a friendly, listening ear.
— My painful circumstances have propelled me to be a more straightforward, honest communicator.
— I am more committed than ever before to be a reliable friend.

__ Because I need people's acceptance, I also intend to extend acceptance to others.

__ I am less inclined now to get caught in fruitless arguments.

__ I am careful not to use tired phrases on people like, "It'll be all right," or "Don't worry, they didn't mean you any harm." I'll not invalidate someone's feelings so easily.

__ My relationship style is less superficial, more in-depth.

__ I feel that I have a better handle than before on limits and expectations in relationships.

__ I am more committed now to maintaining healthy relationship goals.

__ My foundation for security is shifting from external sources to internal sources.

How many did you check? Ideally, you would be able to check all of them, though you should not be surprised if you could not respond to some. The more you could check, the more prepared you probably are in the capacity to reach out to other people who have had emotional struggles.

You Are Not a Perpetual Victim

As you look back upon the circumstances that require your forgiveness, you can admit that you were, indeed, the victim of foul play or poor treatment. As you have contemplated the principles and concepts related to forgiveness, our hope is that you have concluded that though you have been a victim, you need not collapse under the burden of being a perpetual victim. As you forgive, you are also giving yourself permission to disengage from the problems brought upon you by others' insensitivity. This can free you, then, to be an initiator of what is good.

Mark admitted to Dr. Carter that he had felt victimized because the choices made by his daughters lacked common sense yet disrupted his quality of life greatly. "If the truth be fully known," he explained, "this is an extension of the problems I had with my first wife. She's got a real mean streak in her, and she unashamedly helped poison Brianna's and Laurie's attitudes toward me. Had she been more cooperative, my problems with the girls would be much less severe."

Was Mark a victim? In his mind he was. In your mind, you probably were too. Did he have good reason to hold on to his victim status? Given the ongoing nature of the family problems, yes, he could continue to claim victimization if he were so inclined.

"But I don't want to live with the feeling of defeat hanging over me," he said. "Since it's unlikely that my ex-wife will change, and since I'm not sure what the years ahead with my daughters will be like, that leaves the resolution of my feelings up to me."

"I like the way you think!" said Dr. Carter. "What do you have in mind?"

"I'm committed to healthy living. My counseling has taught me to chart a course based on God's will for my life and to stick with it in spite of outside opposition. I've got plenty of life left in me, and I intend to make it count.

"My frustrations with Brianna and Laurie have taught me a few lessons about how *not* to handle family problems. My only good option is to use my experiences for the better. It's going to happen!"

Though Mark had ample reasons to bemoan his family life, he had decided not to let his problems become the defining aspect of his personality. You, too, can make the same determination.

You will know you have come full circle in the forgiveness process when you determine to move forward by giving of yourself to those who can receive the good you have to offer. Rather than being saddled with a victim's ongoing bitterness of insecurity or withdrawal, you can see yourself as one who has plenty to offer others.

As you release yourself from a victim status, seeing instead that you have an increased insight into relationship matters, what can you offer others who have been through trying times? (For instance, "My painful marriage has taught me to give fewer pat answers and give more true listening to others with similar problems," or "Growing up in a difficult family has made me a much more sensitive and patient parent.")

_____

_____

_____

As you commit yourself to forgiveness and as you remain open to helping others who have similarly struggled, keep five key goals in mind that will make you most effective in your dealings with others.

Key 1. Establish Your Identity as a True Encourager

What is your reputation? What are you known for? When you have experienced great disappointment and pain your spirit will naturally be dampened. In time, that disheartened mood can be so pervasive that it seems permanently entrenched. For instance, Mark once told Dr. Carter, "A while back a friend of mine told me I had been consistently moody, as if I were ticked off at the world. Until he pointed it out I wasn't aware that I had let my family problems impact me so strongly. My hurt had become so entrenched that my entire character was influenced by it. My pain had become the defining element in my personality."

Has this ever happened to you? How could your painful experiences negatively affect your overall reputation? (For instance, "Since my husband's affair, I've been very bitter," or "Because of my childhood problems I tend to be known as a timid person.")

_____

_____

_____

You cannot be expected to experience disappointments without also feeling the emotional aftereffects. But don't allow your problems to ultimately dictate who you will be. Like Mark, your difficulties can become the defining element in your personality. Is that what you want?

People in your world need encouragement, just as you do. Perhaps you are familiar with the old proverb: To have a friend you must be a friend. You will be helping others while simultaneously helping yourself when you extend yourself in encouragement to others.

How can you encourage? Let's look at some examples:

- You will find what is right in others and comment regularly about what you like.

- When someone else is hurting you can show them the acceptance they so desperately need.

- You know how painful isolation can feel, so you will initiate contact with others who are in need.

- Rather than letting a mood of gloom settle over your family life you can initiate social activities.

- When someone else discusses personal matters you can ask follow-up questions, showing interest.

- You can appropriately touch other people, demonstrating warmth.

- If you know someone is going through trials, you can regularly contact him or her for an update.

Because you know what it is like to feel burdened, you can use your experiences in a positive way. This is what we mean when we say that your crisis can produce growth. A keener sensitivity can develop within your emotions, meaning you can be all the more valuable in your circle of acquaintances.

As Mark considered his newfound willingness to extend himself to others, he commented, "In the past I had virtually no interest in talking with people about their feelings or needs. I just assumed that personal subjects should be off-limits. Even when I went through my divorce I kept things to myself because I didn't want to draw attention to problems.

"But something snapped in me as I realized my relationship with my daughters was waning," he continued. "Maybe for the first time in my life I realized the importance of staying attuned to others. Right now I'm resolved more than ever to make sure I don't just withdraw from people with an 'I don't care' attitude. People need to connect, and I may as well be the one doing the connecting!"

"So what's new in your relating style that illustrates this new attitude?"

"Well, the main thing is that I'm noticing people's needs more. If someone seems frustrated I ask them about it. If someone's happy I get them to tell me more. If someone seems withdrawn I show an interest in them. I know what it's like to feel out of it, so I'm all the more willing to let people know it's okay to be human and that someone cares."

Think about your current sphere of influence with family, friends, and coworkers. Who needs the encouragement you can offer? Don't assume someone needs no encouragement just because they seem to experience few problems. You never can know what really lies behind the scenes.

In what circumstances could you commit to an encouraging spirit? (For instance, "My younger sister would benefit if I could more openly show love and tolerance," or "My friend had major family problems just as I did, so I can be a source of support, especially around family-oriented holidays.")

_____

_____

_____

Specifically, *how* would you communicate your encouragement? (For instance, "With my sister I could cease criticism and comment on what is right," or "With my friend, I would call more regularly to determine how she's feeling.")

_____

_____

_____

Give to others just as you hope they would give to you.

Key 2. Be a True Listener, Not Just a Teller

Recall your frustrating experiences and focus specifically on the desire you had to feel understood. You wanted someone to register with you, not to direct your next move but just to say, "I hear you, I care."

When you are communicating with someone who similarly needs to feel heard, what form of communication do you use most? The two most common reactions in such circumstances are: (1) You will give advice about how to handle the situation, and (2) You will respond by telling a similar incident in your own life. Have you noticed how unnatural it can sometimes be just to listen, to truly absorb what the other person feels and perceives?

Suppose, for instance, that you've had a major family disagreement and a friend decides to tell you of a similar problem in her life. Picture how easy it is to respond with: "When that happens, you're just going to have to . . ." or "Yeah, when my mother said the same thing to me I told her . . ." What's going on? You're hearing for the purpose of *telling*.

Be willing to hear for the purpose of demonstrating understanding. Slow down. Don't turn someone else's discussion about personal matters into an advice-giving session or into a story-swapping contest. Show that you are absorbing what the other person feels and perceives. For instance:

- When a family member tells you about uncomfortable memories, rather than responding immediately with your memories, comment first on how that person seems to be feeling about the past.

- If a friend discusses how his marital problems are becoming overwhelming, don't just give advice. Comment on how difficult it must be to feel so stressed. Let him talk more.

- If a coworker says she dreads the next meeting with a difficult client, rather than telling her about your own difficult client, ask her how she plans to handle her feelings of uncertainty.

- When your spouse tells you about something good that happened, notice her excitement, then ask her to tell you more about it.

Do you notice the trend in these illustrations? True listening means you will hear with a patient desire to know what the person is processing on the deeper emotional level.

Who in your world needs to feel understood? A relative? A coworker? Someone you see weekly at church? Your kids? Your spouse? Can you recall how strongly you have wanted to feel understood during moments of great stress? Would you be willing to give away what you would like to be given you?

In what circumstances could you be a more in-depth listener? (For instance, "Because I know the frustration of parenting I can be more attuned to my own daughter's frustrations with her kids" or "My friend just lost her job, and I know she's the type who needs to talk out her feelings. I can be the one who will ask her to tell me about it.")

_____

_____

_____

What personal habits will you need to set aside in order to be the most effective listener? (For instance, "I talk too much, so I'd need to talk less and hear more," or "I'd need to refrain from giving advice and notice feelings more fully.")

How would your gift of understanding toward someone else ultimately help *you?* (For instance, "For so long I've felt unnecessary, so being a listener would help me feel useful," or "It would remind me that my past struggles have not been experienced completely in vain.")

Your listening skills will complement your intentions to be an encourager. Without saying the actual words, your listening tells the other person, "You're important," or "What you perceive makes sense." By giving the gift of understanding there is an increased likelihood that you will be rewarded with an improved friendship and deepening love. That may not be your goal, but it can be a welcome by-product.

Key 3. Share Your Experiences When Appropriate

As Mark talked with Dr. Carter about his changing outlook on relationships, he commented, "Man, I can see that I've been communicating with all the wrong tools. I'm one of those people who almost immediately jumps in with advice if someone talks about personal problems. And it's real common for me to say, 'That reminds me of . . .' Are you suggesting that I should just keep my mouth shut and not bore people with stories about my own problems?"

"Not necessarily. What I'm saying is that it's usually good to establish your encouragement and your understanding *first*. Once that's done, it may be appropriate to share your similar experiences with others, but the result of it will be different. Your personal revelations will be less self-focused in purpose and more ministering in purpose."

"I like that," he said, "though I never would have used the word *ministering.*"

"There are moments when we each need to be open with one another about our ups and downs," explained Dr. Carter, "because it can help others feel less isolated or less inadequate. The Bible tells us to bear one another's burdens and confess to one another. When we do, we become servants, and we demonstrate humility and authenticity. People want to know that you are real, and when they do they'll usually be real in return."

Opening himself up in true vulnerability was difficult for Mark since he tended to maintain a tough, macho veneer. But it was rewarding. As he let his human side be seen, he felt that he was more successful at establishing substance in his relationships. Depth replaced superficiality in his closest friendships. "It's funny how it works," he said, "but it took some really painful experiences to get me to be open. I'm not glad I've been through my family frustrations, but I *am* glad for what I'm learning as a direct result of my problems."

How about you? Could you say the same thing? Experiencing pain was not in your plans. Being rejected or manipulated is not what you wanted. Yet, would you be willing to expose your feelings and experiences if it could help someone else through his or her struggles?

In what situation would it be helpful for you to openly disclose your problematic situations? (For instance, "My friend has been physically abused by her husband, and I could share with her how I handled the same problem in my past," or "My brother is

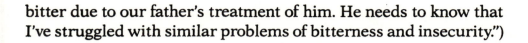

bitter due to our father's treatment of him. He needs to know that I've struggled with similar problems of bitterness and insecurity.")

_____

_____

_____

How might you be required to realign your priorities in order to be appropriately open and vulnerable? (For instance, "I'd need to view my self-disclosure as an act of ministry," or "I'd talk about my experiences with the intent of deepening my relationships.")

_____

_____

_____

Some people will balk at the notion of openly exposing their problems, saying that self-disclosure could create more problems than it would solve. Others cannot be trusted; they may refuse to respond with acceptance or confidentiality. Unfortunately, that may be true in some instances. Be careful, though, not to retreat to the opposite extreme of disclosing nothing. Someone needs to hear from you. Someone can be helped by you, and when you become helpful, your past problems will not seem as devastating. Be careful in your decision to disclose, but not so much that you deprive others and yourself from the benefits that can be found through openness.

Key 4. Be Committed to Authenticity

Following closely on the heels of the willingness to be open is the commitment to authenticity, the willingness to be real. Too often when people have experienced heartache and personal trauma there is a tendency to cover up. Through the years we have observed how people have locked themselves into self-imposed prisons by covering their pain with disingenuous behaviors. For instance:

- A woman who was sexually abused by a relative feels the need to fake it when in the abuser's presence at a family gathering.

- In a social setting a man assumes he's supposed to act as if his life is wonderful even though he is going through severe family strains.

- A grandmother is experiencing problems with her misbehaving grandkids, but she feels she can't let anyone know how disappointed she feels.

- A dad doesn't know how to act around his teenagers as he realizes they resent the way their mother disciplines them.

- A friend assumes a man is doing well on the job, but he is not. He does not feel comfortable, though, in going into detail about work problems.

When have you been in a circumstance in which your problems, caused by others, have left you feeling that you couldn't afford to be real? (For instance, "I despise my husband's social habits, but I feel that I have to put on a front in public," or "When I visit my parents I'm not allowed to say anything about our long history of conflicts.")

_____

_____

_____

How does this "requirement" of phoniness negatively affect your emotions? (For instance, "I become all the more bitter," or "I withdraw in silent disgust.")

_____

_____

_____

When you are in a situation where you are reminded of your pain-producing problems, there are two extremes to avoid: (1) The extreme of completely suppressing the real you, and (2) The extreme of overly displaying your negative reactions regarding those problems.

For instance, when Mark discussed with his friend his problems regarding his daughters, he had been tempted to pretend that it was a minor problem that didn't really bother him. He later realized he could go to the other extreme of lambasting them by recalling how rude they had acted toward him. "I decided not to take either path," he reflected to Dr. Carter. "The approach I'm taking is to say little that is negative about my problems with Brianna and Laurie when most people ask me the typical questions about how they're doing. However, with my closest friends and with people who need encouragement because of similar pain, I've concluded that it can be helpful to talk about my feelings, not for the sake of gaining sympathy, but for the sake of helping them be open and honest with me, if that's what they need to do."

Mark realized that his commitment to genuineness helped ease his emotional duress. He had decided it was necessary with key people to communicate, "I've got my humanness, but I'm going to survive in spite of it." He matched his commitment to authenticity with a similar commitment to diplomacy, meaning he would refrain from complaining at his daughters' expense. This made his choice to forgive easier since he was being honest while he was also helping his close friends to more honestly disclose their feelings too.

When could you afford to be more genuine about your real feelings and experiences? (For instance, "When I'm with my best friend I won't need to pretend my marriage is great, because it really isn't," or "I don't have to agree to have lunch with my mother every time she suggests it because in doing so I'm covering up my feelings of hurt with her.")

_____

_____

_____

"I've decided that when people make the effort to get to know me, they're not just going to hear about all the pleasant and fluffy parts of my life. I'm going to let them see me, bumps and all." In deciding to be more genuine, Mark was hoping to pave the way for others to remove their masks as well. "No need to put on false fronts," he explained, "if it also encourages someone else to do the same. I want people to feel they can be honest with me, so I'll set the pace by being honest myself."

How can your commitment to authenticity and honesty be an encouragement to others? (For instance, "My sister has hurt as I have, and it would be good for her to know we can have heart-to-heart discussions," or "I'm learning that my openness makes others feel they will be accepted by me.")

_____

_____

_____

Key 5. Share with Others the Keys to Forgiveness

When you commit to being a genuine, open encourager, be prepared for deeper communication with key people in your life. Most likely you will establish a reputation as approachable, and you will readily find that many people are looking for someone who will hear them and understand. To keep it balanced, you don't have to try to become a counselor, yet you can be of help by letting others know what works for you. Your ability to overcome difficulties can be an inspiration to others.

Mark told Dr. Carter about a Christmas card he had received from the friend who also had problems with his adult kids. "Normally, men don't send Christmas cards to each other, and when we do we usually just sign our name and that's it." The doctor smiled knowingly as Mark continued. "James wrote a nice note in this card telling me how much he treasured my friendship and how much it meant to him that I would take an interest in him. I *really* liked getting that card because I knew he meant it."

"It reminds you of how isolated we can feel even when we're surrounded by many people. Sounds to me as though James was ready for a friend like you who would be open. You've both gained because of your determination to be involved."

Think of someone who needs you. How could that person benefit by your presence in his or her life? (For instance, "I have a friend who had family problems similar to mine, and I know she'll appreciate it if I talk with her as someone who knows what it's like," or "If my brother could see how I've come to terms with our father, it would help him do the same.")

_____

_____

_____

Be open about the principles that have helped you forgive. For instance, if you've been unbalanced in your angry responses, admit it. If you've developed a controlling manner, discuss how you're going to improve. Your vulnerability can pave the way for someone else.

What principles of forgiveness have been most valuable to you as you have sought to overcome your hurts? (For instance, "Realizing I needed to react less and initiate my own plan has been a key for me," or "Learning how to keep better boundaries as part of my healing has kept me from bitterly clinging to my past.")

_____

_____

_____

Can you share your principles and insights with others? Be careful not to be preachy or to sound like someone who has perfected life, yet realize that your experiences can help them.

Forgiveness is not always an easily attained goal. Trying to come to terms with your pain can stretch you beyond your comfort zones. As you share the principles of forgiveness with someone in the same boat, you will find that your commitment to these principles will be fortified, and you will feel inspired to know others will find healing with you and perhaps because of you.

About the Authors

Frank Minirth, M.D., is the president and proprietor of The Minirth Clinic in Richardson, Texas. He was cofounder of the Minirth Meier New Life Clinics. He is a diplomate of the American Board of Psychiatry and Neurology and received his M.D. from the University of Arkansas.

Dr. Minirth has coauthored more than thirty books, including *The Power of Memories, The Headache Book, Love Is a Choice, Love Hunger, The Father Book, Things That Go Bump in the Night, The Anger Workbook, The Path to Serenity, Worry-Free Living, Happiness Is a Choice, The Freedom from Depression Workbook*, and *You Can!* He resides in Plano, Texas, with his wife and five daughters.

Les Carter, Ph.D., is a nationally known expert in the field of Christian counseling, with more than twenty years in private practice. He is a psychotherapist with The Minirth Clinic.

Dr. Carter earned his B.A. from Baylor University and his M.Ed. and Ph.D. from North Texas State University. He is the author or coauthor of fourteen books, including *Distant Partner, The Freedom from Depression Workbook, The Anger Workbook, Imperative People, Reflecting the Character of Christ*, and *Broken Vows*. Dr. Carter and his family reside in Dallas, Texas.

CPSIA information can be obtained at www.ICGtesting.com
Printed in the USA
LVOW110430190612

286647LV00002B/6/A